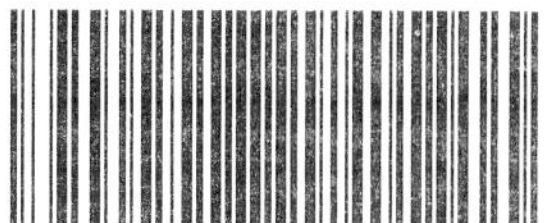

GOD'S MIDDLEMEN

GOD'S MIDDLEMEN

A HaBaD Retrospective

Stories of Mystical Rabbis

REUVEN ALPERT

with an Introduction by

BEZALEL NAOR

White Cloud Press
Ashland, Oregon

White Cloud Press, PO Box 3400, Ashland, OR 97520. Phone/fax 541-488-6415.
Web site: http://www.jeffnet.org/whitecloud

Printed in the United States

99 98 98 5 4 3 2 1

Photo credits: Rabbi Zevi Yehuda Hakohen Kook—from David Samson and Tzvi Fishman, *Torat Eretz Yisrael* (Jerusalem, 1991); Yaakov Alperowitz—from Jordan S. Alpert, *The Alperts and Cohens of Bangor, Maine* (San Francisco, 1990); Rabbi Nachman Kowalsky—courtesy of Rabbi Sholem B. Kowalsky; Rabbi Baruch Naeh—from *Kfar Chabad* magazine, Nov. 15, 1989; Rabbi Shlomo Carlebach—courtesy of Neila Carlebach; Rabbi Shlomo Twersky—photo by Ed Bernstein, Bernstein Studios, Denver; Rabbis Menahem Mendel Schneersohn I, Shalom Baer Schneersohn, Joseph Isaac Schneersohn, and Menahem Mendel Schneerson II—from *Challenge* (London, 1970).

Quotation on p. 73 from *The Diaries of Judith Malina 1947-1957* (New York: Grove Press, 1984), p. 422.

Cover design by Impact Graphics, Medford, Oregon

LIBRARY OF CONGRESS CATALOGING-IN-PUBLICATION DATA

Alpert, Reuven,
God's middlemen : A Habad retrospective : stories of mystical rabbis / Reuven Alpert ; with an introduction by Bezalel Naor.
p. cm.
Includes bibliographical references.
ISBN 1-883991-17-X
1. Habad--Anecdotes. 2. Hasidim--Anecdotes. 3. Rabbis--Anecdotes. 4. Alpert, Reuven--Anecdotes. I. Na'or, Betsal'el.
II. Title.
BM198.54.A43 1997
296.8'3222'0922-dc21
[B] 97-29964
CIP

Contents

Appreciation

A heartfelt note of appreciation to Steven Scholl, publisher of White Cloud Press, who ventured into the field of Jewish spirituality—a field foreign to him—and with patience, dedication, and tolerance succeeded in crafting a book beyond its authors' expectations.

Reuven Alpert Bezalel Naor

Note to the Reader

God's Middlemen is divided into two sections: Bezalel Naor's scholarly survey of the HaBaD movement, followed by Reuven Alpert's engaging tales of HaBaD rabbis. The style of these two sections is very different but we feel they both add to our understanding of the history and current developments within the HaBaD community. If you are more interested in great Jewish storytelling, you may want to begin with Alpert's stories of the rabbis. If you are new to Jewish mysticism and the HaBaD movement, you may wish to orient yourself with Rabbi Naor's survey of HaBaD Hasidism.

The Editors

The Founders of Hasidism

Israel b. Eliezer Baal Shem Tov, Founder of Hasidism
(1698 or 1700-1760)

Dov Baer b. Abraham of Mezhirech
(?-1772)

The Schneerso(h)n Dynasty

descendants of Shneur Zalman of Liady, founder of HaBaD (Wisdom, Understanding, Knowledge) School of Hasidism

Shneur Zalman b. Baruch of Liady, Founder of HaBaD School
(1745-1813)

Dov Baer b. Shneur Zalman of Lubavitch
(1773-1827)

Menahem Mendel b. Shalom Shachna of Lubavitch (*Zemah Zedek*)
(1789-1866)

Sons of *Zemah Zedek*:

Judah Leib of Kopyst
(1811-1866)

Hayyim Shneur Zalman of Liady
(1814?-1880)

Samuel of Lubavitch
(1834-1882)

Sons of Judah Leib of Kopyst:

Solomon Zalman of Kopyst
(1830-1900)

Shalom Dov Baer of Retchitsa
(1840?-1908)

Shemariah Noah of Bobroisk
(1846-1926)

Son of Hayyim Shneur Zalman of Liady:

Isaac Dov Baer of Liady
(1835-1910)

Descendants of Samuel of Lubavitch:

Shalom Dov Baer b. Samuel of Lubavitch (1860-1920)
Joseph Isaac b. Shalom Dov Baer of Lubavitch (1880-1950)
Menahem Mendel b. Levi Isaac of Lubavitch (1902-1994)*

* Menaham Mendel was the son-in-law of Joseph Isaac, and thus not a direct descendant of Samuel of Lubavitch

Introduction

by Bezalel Naor

1. Essence of Hasidism: Enchantment

Do you remember as a child asking your mother if some object is alive, only to be told, to your disappointment, that it is not? As you grew up, you discovered that more and more aspects of reality are "not alive." Hasidic teaching would be something like a process of reeducation whereby as time progressed, you would increasingly discover that the universe surrounding you is full of "light and life" (*or ve-hiyyut*), teeming with divine vitality. It would be the equivalent of your mother (this time a surrogate mother or "rebbe") answering "yes" to your primal question. Yes, it is alive![1]

In contemporary literature, this perception of the universe as vital is referred to as "enchantment." What your parent did when he or she broke the spell was "disenchantment." Myself, I prefer the term "animation," from *anima* or soul. The opposite process would be "deanimation." But "enchantment" has merit to it as it derives from the Latin root *cantare*, to sing. The enchanted universe is a singing universe. The best example from the American cultural scene I can think of to illustrate this is the Tikki Hut at Disneyland. When first seated in this replica of a Polynesian hut, one's initial reaction is: "How am I going to survive the boredom of the next half hour?" No sooner have the lights dimmed than the entire thatched structure begins to vibrate with energy, as out of hidden recesses birds of every imaginable description join in a chorus. At the end of his Tale of the Changelings, Rabbi Nahman of Braslav has a throne like that, in which all the hewn figures come alive and begin to sing in unison. In Rabbi Nahman's story, countless individuals had wandered into the royal garden, but the wonderful orchestra could be heard only by the prodigal son. Only the true prince possesses the key of wisdom to make an otherwise inanimate display come alive.

Hasidism's founder, Israel Baal Shem Tov, of blessed memory, commented on the verse in Genesis:

> Your word, *Let there be a firmament in the midst of the waters etc.*, these very letters constantly stand in the firmament of the heavens, to enliven them .[2]

Baal Shem Tov's spiritual grandson, Shneur Zalman of Liady, extended this teaching:

> And so in regard to all the creations in all the worlds, upper and lower, even this material earth and the inanimate order . . . This is what ARI (Rabbi Isaac Luria), of blessed memory, wrote, that even in the inanimate, such as stones, earth and water, there is a soul and a spiritual vitality.[3]

For many years it was in vogue in scientific circles to regard this vitalistic worldview as the product of a primitive mind. Today, with the revolutionary advances in modern physics, the tables have been turned: The old mechanistic science has been relegated to the scrap heap of discarded ideas, while Baal Shem Tov's vision of a world pulsating with energy is the cutting edge of science.

2. Intellectual Origins of Hasidism: Saadyah / Spinoza

Israel Baal Shem Tov was born in the hamlet of Okop, Podolia in the year 1698 or 1700. He died in 1760 in the somewhat larger town of Medzibezh[4] (today Ukraine). His entire life was spent in a backwater province in the shadow of the Carpathian Mountains. Yet this relatively obscure figure, concerning whom we have scant hard facts, was to bequeath to humanity a teaching which to this day engages the minds of great thinkers and religious philosophers.

Where did Baal Shem Tov's worldview come from? He himself said that he was the reincarnation of the early Jewish philosopher Saadyah, who lived in Egypt and Babylonia in the 900s. It was attested that he would study Saadyah's writings.[5]

This self-appraisal of Baal Shem Tov must be taken with the utmost gravity. In *Ben Porat Yosef* by his Boswell, Rabbi Jacob Joseph Hakohen of Polonnoye, we find two references to Saadyah. The first, which is difficult to pin to anything concrete in Saadyah's writings, lies within the realm of ethics:

> I heard from my teacher [Baal Shem Tov], of blessed memory, in the name of Rabbenu Saadyah Gaon, that primarily man was created in this world to break his natural evil character traits.[6]

Nothing very revolutionary about that. The next quote from Saadyah has merited considerable scholarly attention:

> I heard from my teacher [Baal Shem Tov], of blessed memory, in the name of Rabbenu Saadyah Gaon, that a man should desire all the material things and thereby (*mi-tokho*) come to desire Torah and the service of God.[7]

This statement bespeaks an ardor worthy of a mystic tradition. The problem with the attribution from a critical stance, is that Saadyah mentions this approach only to discredit it.[8] Zweifel,[9] who was the first historian to take the pains to locate the reference in Saadyah's philosophic magnum opus, *Kitab al-Amanat w'al I'tiqadat* (*The Book of Beliefs and Opinions*), unfortunately used a secondary work *Keter Shem Tov*[10] rather than the primary source *Ben Porat Yosef.* This led him to the mistaken impression that Baal Shem Tov intended some sort of hermeneutics, whereby one would reason from the minor to the major, from desire of the material to desire of the spiritual. Of course, Baal Shem Tov's approach was not rational but rather experiential. The experience of earthly desire would bring to desire of the divine. Mendel Piekarz, who paints a broad canvass of the period, points out that Baal Shem Tov's creative "misreading" of an earlier text is typical of his contemporaries.[11]

Saadyah may not have been the best source; the notion that desire of a woman, specifically, is a prerequisite for divine service, was clearly enunciated—and approvingly—by the fourteenth century kabbalist Rabbi Isaac of Acre.[12]

The two direct references to Saadyah at best reflect the periphery of Baal Shem Tov's teaching. What of the essence of that teaching, namely the peculiar pantheistic belief? Can that be traced to the writings of Saadyah?

David Cohen[13] (the so-called Nazirite) has pointed out the following passage in Saadyah's *Beliefs and Opinions* as evocative of an immantentist theology:

> "But how is it possible for our minds to conceive the thought of God's presence everywhere so that no place would be vacant of His presence?" My answer is that God existed before there was any such thing as space. If, therefore, the existence of many different localities could have brought about a division among the parts of the Creator's personality, He would not have created them. Again, if the various material objects would have taken away space from Him or a certain amount of space, He would not have had to produce them. Since, then, that is the case, His existence after His creation of all the bodies must be exactly as it was before He

> had created them without any change or division or concealment or interruption, but, rather, as Scripture puts it: *Can any hide himself in secret places that I shall not see him? saith the Lord. Do not I fill heaven and earth?* (Jeremiah 23:24)
>
> Now let me make this a little more comprehensible, and say that if we had not been accustomed to noting that certain walls do not cut off sound, and had we not been in the habit of observing that glass does not screen the light, and had we not known that the light of the sun is not affected adversely by the filth that exists in the world, we would have been rather surprised at the above-mentioned. All these [commonplace] marvels serve, therefore, as a corroboration of the validity of our idea of God.[14]

Scholars who strive to be objective cannot help but be struck by the similarities between the philosophical system of Spinoza and Baal Shem Tov's Hasidism. This was the finding of such diverse researchers as Eliezer Zweifel, Abraham Isaac Kook, and Martin Buber.[15] Yet, not even the boldest of theoreticians would venture that there was a direct influence of the seventeenth century Amsterdam philosopher upon the eigtheenth century East European wonderworker. Furthermore, there is a fundamental difference between the two philosophies. For Spinoza, the identification of God and Nature is total and exhaustive, there is only the immanent God; whereas in Baal Shem Tov's vision, God is both immanent and transcendent. "He fills all worlds and surrounds all worlds."[16] In modern theologic jargon this would be the difference between "pantheism" (all is God) and "panentheism" (all in God).[17]

3. Possible Parallels to Hasidism: Swedenborg, Emerson, and Thoreau

As far as parallels go, it strikes one as significant that Israel Baal Shem Tov (1698 or 1700-1760) and the Swedish mystic Emanuel Swedenborg (1688-1772) were contemporaries. Both excelled at clairvoyance, nonliteral interpretation of Bible and shamanistic incursions into the spiritual realm. Are these two manifestations of a single Zeitgeist?[18]

American readers will remember that Swedenborgian spirituality guided the nineteenth century New England school of Transcendentalists, of whom the most famous figures are Emerson and Thoreau. Emerson, in particular, was fascinated by Swedenborg's theory of Correspondence, whereby events on the material plane correspond to their spiritual analogs—an outlook remarkably similar to much hasidic teaching.

Having mentioned Thoreau, let us state that both Baal Shem Tov and later his great-grandson, Nahman of Braslav attributed their spiritual success to years spent in seclusion in the woods.[19] Though it did not originate the saying, Hasidism made *Ha-teva bi-gematria elohim*, "Nature is (numerically) equivalent to God," its clarion call.[20]

4. History of Hasidism

Israel Baal Shem Tov

The founder of Hasidism, Israel Baal Shem Tov lived his first thirty-six years as a *nistar*, a hidden individual. Of his parents, Eliezer and Sarah, we know almost nothing. Israel was orphaned at an early age. His father's dying words to him were: "*Yisraelnu*, fear only God, not man." A remarkable message to entrust to one so young.

Israel worked for a while as a *belfer* (or *behelfer*), whose job it was to carry children to and from religious instruction. There are numerous legends concerning his adventures protecting the children entrusted to his care from both physical and metaphysical dangers.[21] This cycle of stories is reminiscent of those the rabbis told concerning Moses' concern for the sheep he tended before the theophany at the Burning Bush. The stories point up that the noble traits of leadership exhibit themselves early in life.

Israel would marry Hannah, the sister of the scholar Rabbi Gershon Kitover, which caused considerable consternation to the latter, as Baal Shem Tov was still to outer appearances a hopeless simpleton. In later years, after Baal Shem Tov's self-revelation, the roles between brothers-in-law would be reversed with Baal Shem Tov acting as mentor to Rabbi Gershon Kitover. But you can imagine how tense were the early relations between the two men.

After their marriage, a routine developed whereby Baal Shem Tov would spend the week up in the hills digging clay for a profession, returning home to his wife only on Sabbaths.

At age thirty-six the seeming dullard revealed himself to the world as a spiritual authority. From then until his death, one pictures Baal Shem Tov constantly in motion. If your agenda is *tikkunim* (corrections) and *yihudim* (unifications), there is plenty of work to be done. There are orphans to be married, widows to be comforted, sick to be cured, captives to be ransomed, demons to be exorcised and—if you are the *Baal Shem Tov* ("Master of the Good Name")—there are even dead to be resurrected.[22]

Legend has it that Saturday night immediately after the conclusion of the Sabbath, Baal Shem Tov and his disciples would hitch the horses up to the wagon and take off in whichever direction the spirit moved the animals. Allowing the wagon to travel on "automatic pilot" brought them to their divinely ordained destination, where inevitably a mission of cosmic proportions would unfold.

The Jewish community was not unanimous in its applaud for Baal Shem Tov. This was due as much to his criticism of the rabbis of his generation for their egotism (a theme with which the *Toledot* of his amanuensis Jacob Joseph Hakohen of Polonnoye is replete), as to the unorthodox method by which he effected these *tikkunim* or mystical corrections of the soul. The following episode illustrates our point:

Once a woman came to the Baal Shem Tov to receive an amulet for a certain illness. The master said if she would give him the amount of fifty rubles he would give her the amulet. The woman travelled home and after having sold all her worldly possessions arrived at the sum of thirty rubles. She returned to the master and told him she could muster only thirty rubles. He refused to give her the amulet.

Not to be deterred, the woman then travelled to the Council of the Four Lands (then under the presidency of Rabbi David of Ostroh) and asked that they raise on her behalf the outstanding twenty rubles to present to the *zaddik* (righteous man). When the rabbis of the council heard her plea, they were outraged and summoned Baal Shem Tov to immediately appear in court. The master complied. At the entrance to the court he stood and smoked his pipe until the building filled with smoke and not one of the judges could open his mouth to utter a syllable, as the awe of the *Shekhinah* (divine presence) fell upon them. Then the master strode over to the Gaon (Talmudic genius) Rabbi David and said to him: "David, David, come and I will show you the new heavens and earth I created by virtue of the *yihudim* (unifications) I effected while smoking my pipe." The master showed him and Rabbi David fainted away. When he was revived, he told his associates: *Mit Gott alein tcheppet nisht*! "With God Himself do not start up!" "Believe me, this is no human being."

Now the woman as a result of her great desire to give the *zaddik* what he asked for, miraculously became exceedingly wealthy. And this had been the intention of the holy man all along.[23]

There were two clocks in Baal Shem Tov's home. He told his disciples that at the time of his soul's expiration they would note that both clocks ground to a halt. After Baal Shem Tov washed his hands, one clock stopped. Not wishing to cause the dying man anxiety, the hasidim blocked his view of the clock. Thereupon Baal Shem Tov proceeded to speak of the ascent of the souls in the Garden of Eden. When moments later Baal Shem Tov's pure soul left his body, the second clock stopped ticking as well, just as he had predicted.[24]

By the time of his death on the second day of Shavuot, 1760, Israel Baal Shem Tov had become a legend. In this century there was a heated debate between two learned professors whether the essence of Hasidism is contained in the tales or in the formal teachings. Martin Buber believed the anecdotal material is crucial to the hasidic experience; Gershom Scholem parried that only through a systematic examination of the formal doctrines could one come to a proper understanding of Hasidism.[25] Perhaps the tales and the theories stand in relation to one another as body and soul.[26] The Baal Shem Tov speaks to us as eloquently through his actions, through his journeys and wanderings on behalf of the downtrodden as through the formal teachings recorded by his disciples.

To once again draw a comparison to Moses, the leader would not be succeeded by his son but rather by his student. Baal Shem Tov's son, Zevi, must have been a lackluster individual. His sister Adel, on the other hand, emerges as a powerful personality. Her two sons, the elder, Baruch of Medzibezh, a dominant disposition whom we will encounter later vis-à-vis Shneur Zalman of Liady, and the younger, Moses Hayyim Efraim of Sudylkow (who recorded many teachings of his grandfather in his book *Degel Mahaneh Efraim*) became leaders of the third generation of Hasidism. Their sister Feige would bear a son Nahman, great-grandson of Baal Shem Tov, who has been described as the "genius of Hasidism."

DOV BAER OF MEZHIRECH

The reins of leadership were entrusted to a lame preacher (or *maggid*) named Dov Baer of Mezhirech, who made Baal Shem Tov's acquaintance toward the end of the master's career (to the dismay of the aforementioned Jacob Joseph of Polonnoye). If Baal Shem Tov was peripatetic, the lifestyle of the Great Maggid, as he was called, can only be typified as stationary. The focus of attention shifted from "glen and dale" to the studyhouse. Dov Baer was interested in producing students who in turn, would further promulgate the ideas to the masses. It is possible that not only the site of Hasidism's spiritual laboratory shifted, but also the thrust of the teaching. If before the theme was communion with nature, now most evident was a brutal, unrelenting assault upon the ego. By the time interloper Solomon Maimon arrived on the scene, on his way from talmudic studies in Nesvizh, Lithuania to the salons of Berlin, the message of Mezhirech (one from which the Maggid would not budge) was that of *bittul ha-yesh* (annihilation of the self), or as Maimon expressed it in his German autobiography, *Selbstzernichtung.*[27]

Maimon has recorded for posterity what the Sabbath was like in Mezhirech:

> On Sabbath I went to this solemn meal, and there found a large number of respectable men who had gathered together from various quarters. At length the great man appeared, his awe-inspiring figure clothed in white satin. Even his shoes and snuffbox were white, this being among the kabbalists the color of grace. He greeted each newcomer with "Shalom." We sat down to table and during the meal a solemn silence reigned. After the meal was over, the superior struck up a solemn inspiring melody, held his hand for some time upon his brow, and then began to call out, "Z . . . of H . . ., M . . . of R, S.M. of N . . .," and so on. Each newcomer was thus called by his own name and the name of his residence, which excited no little astonishment. Each as he was called recited some verse of the Holy Scriptures. Thereupon the superior began to deliver a sermon for which the verses recited served as text, so that although they were disconnected verses taken from different parts of Scripture they were combined with as much skill as if they had formed a single whole. What was still more extraordinary, every one of the newcomers believed that he discovered in that part of the sermon which was founded on his verse something that had special reference to the facts of his own spiritual life. At this we were of course greatly astonished.[28]

What makes Maimon's testimony so significant is that it is not the deposition of a hasid, but rather of a skeptic who would go on to

Koenigsberg to become an authoritative interpreter of Kant's critical philosophy.

After having spent a few years studying under the Maggid, students would scatter to every direction of the European continent. Two brothers, Shmelke and Pinhas Horowitz accepted rabbinical posts in Western Europe, an area especially inhospitable to Hasidism. Shmelke settled in Nikolsburg, Moravia and Pinhas in Frankfort. Another disciple of the Maggid, Levi Isaac, still remembered by the masses for his love of the Jewish People, settled in Berdichev, Ukraine (after having been chased out of Pinsk by the opponents of Hasidism, or *mitnagdim*, as they were called). Rabbi Elimelekh of Lizhansk planted the seed of Hasidism in Poland. Rabbi Aaron of Karlin, a hardy soul, brought Hasidism to the resistant soil of Lithuania. In the earliest reports of the czarist government concerning the nascent movement, the hasidim are referred to as members of the "Karliner" sect.[29] Another master who established his seat in the Ukraine, was Rabbi Menahem Nahum of Chernobyl (a city infamous in our day as the site of the terrible nuclear "meltdown"), an itinerant preacher who followed in Baal Shem Tov's footsteps, travelling from place to place to raise funds for the ransom of captives.

Hasidism was not without its adversaries. The spread of the movement met with stiff resistance from the rabbinic establishment (the *Mitnagdim*) on the one hand, and from the proponents of secular enlightenment (the so-called *Maskilim*), on the other.[30] Both groups were not above denouncing the leaders of the Hasidic movement. Despite all opposition, the movement spread like wildfire. Inspired by charismatic leaders, Hasidism had become a grassroots movement of spiritual revival. Baal Shem Tov had acted as a magnifying glass focusing rays of divine light upon the Jewish People whose souls caught fire. Indeed, *hitlahavut*, the hasidic term for ecstasy, derives from *lahav*, a flame.[31] At the turn of the nineteenth century, the Hegelian philosopher, Nahman Krochmal noted with consternation that the hasidic sect, previously restricted to "the caves of Wallachia, the steppes of the Ukraine and the villages perched on the Hungarian border," had begun to make inroads into the major cities and seats of learning: Lvov (Lemberg), Brody, Vilna, Brisk (Brest-Litovsk).[32]

Perhaps the greatest of the Maggid's disciples was a young *Litvak* (Lithuanian) with a blond beard, named Shneur Zalman. The young man had reached a spiritual crossroads in his life: He had already completed study of the entire Talmud at age eighteen.[33] Now twenty years old, he must decide whether he should head north to Vilna to further perfect his Talmudic expertise in the study halls of the "Jerusalem of Lithuania," or south to Mezhirech to explore the mysteries of the spirit. Luckily for us, Shneur Zalman wended his way to the Maggid of Mezhirech.

Rabbi Dov Baer had an astute eye for sizing up and developing young talent. He put the *Litvak* in tandem with his very own son, Abraham "the Angel" (*malakh*). Shneur Zalman would hone Abraham's skills in Talmud and Abraham would uncover for Shneur Zalman the mysteries of Baal Shem Tov's teaching.

Eventually, Rabbi Dov Baer would charge his brilliant student with creating a new code of Jewish law, a *Shulhan Arukh* tailor-made for the Jews of the time.[34]

Beyond that, the far-roving eye of the Maggid foresaw that one day this disciple would be the one to bridge the gap between the heady intellectualism of his Lithuanian birthplace and the oceanic spirituality to which he was now being exposed in Podolia. Out of that very creative tension Shneur Zalman would forge his specific brand of Hasidism, HaBaD (acronym for *Hokhmah, Binah, Daat*—Wisdom, Understanding and Knowledge).

After having led the hasidim for thirteen years, the Maggid passed away on the 19th of Kislev, 1773. Legend has it that when it came time to immerse the holy Maggid's body in the *mikveh* (ritual bath) for purification, the disciples drew lots to determine which limb each should carry.[35] Symbolically, Shneur Zalman of Liady received the head, Levi

Isaac of Berdichev, the heart, and Menahem Nahum of Chernobyl, the thighs. (Menahem Nahum excelled in sexual purity.)

The mantle of leadership now fell to the Maggid's son Abraham "the Angel." When he passed away prematurely at age thirty-six in 1776, direction of the group was assumed by the Maggid's major disciple, Rabbi Menahem Mendel of Horodok and Vitebsk. As for the Maggid's physical descendants, they were not devoid of spiritual gifts. Two generations later, Abraham's grandson, Israel (Friedman) founded the regal Ryzhin dynasty.

In 1774, Rabbis Menahem Mendel and Shneur Zalman travelled together to Vilna to appease "the Gaon" (genius), Rabbi Elijah, who was the most authoritative foe of Hasidism. There are different accounts of what ensued. (Some say the Gaon's mother forbade him to meet with the hasidic delegation.) One thing is certain: The Gaon refused to countenance the two hasidic leaders. As the Gaon was a great kabbalist and visionary in his own right, it is impossible that he opposed Hasidism on rationalist grounds. What doctrinal differences regarding the correct interpretation of Kabbalah divided them, remains a moot point. As the meeting between the two camps never materialized, the Gaon never "lay his cards on the table," as the expression goes.

In 1777, Rabbi Menahem Mendel and Rabbi Abraham Katz of Kalisk led a group of 300 hasidim to the Holy Land where they eventually sank roots in the Galilean city of Tiberias. Rabbi Shneur Zalman travelled with them overland as far as Mogilov on the river Dnestr. There it was decided he would remain behind in Russia to maintain a life-support system for the spiritual adepts in their new home, while providing guidance to the hasidim still in Russia. In years to come, the *mitnagdim* would cite Rabbi Shneur Zalman's fund-raising activities on behalf of the hasidic colonists to trump up charges that he was in collusion with the Turkish enemy. (Palestine was then an Ottoman satrap.) Those charges culminated in the *Alter Rebbe*'s imprisonment in Saint Petersburg.

SHNEUR ZALMAN OF LIADY

Faced with the realization that he would not be one of the elect to dwell in the holy atmosphere of the Galilee, epicenter of kabbalistic activity for centuries, Rabbi Shneur Zalman applied himself to developing Hasidism as he understood it. First in Liozno and later in Liady (the town usually associated with his name) he established formal academies of learning (*hadarim*). There young men would be trained in Talmud and also the classics of Jewish Philosophy, but above all, there they would imbibe the arcane discipline of Hasidism. Helping him in the labor of "processing" souls was his son Dov Baer, who from a tender age was impressed into this service.

To further spread the word of Hasidism, in 1796, Rabbi Shneur Zalman authored a work which he entitled *Sefer shel Benonim*, "Book of the (Spiritual) Middle Class," now referred to as *Tanya*, after the book's beginning word.[36] Hasidism had become unwieldy. It was simply no longer possible to counsel intimately the hundreds of thousands into which the movement had grown.[37] Just as *Shulhan Arukh* would provide guidance in the outer, practical observance of Judaism, so *Sefer shel Benonim* would offer the masses direction concerning the interior life.

Now Rabbi Shneur Zalman comes under blistering attack from his peers. Though in his introduction to *Sefer shel Benonim* he bent over backward to defer to the authority of the rabbis in the Holy Land, publication of the work provoked a swift and outspoken reaction from Rabbi Abraham Katz of Kalisk (who assumed leadership of the hasidim in Tiberias after Rabbi Menahem Mendel's passing in 1788). It was apparent to Shneur Zalman's colleagues that he had embarked on a new way, one which they could not endorse. Abraham of Kalisk's letter to Shneur Zalman has been preserved:

> As for myself, I am displeased by His Honor having put the sun in a sheath, garbing the words of our master, the holy rabbi of Mezhirech—which are the words of the holy rabbi Baal Shem Tov—in the idiom of the holy rabbi ARI [Isaac Luria], of blessed memory.[38]

How dare Rabbi Shneur Zalman mix languages? Hasidism had created a fresh idiom. Who was this upstart who would attempt to synthesize Baal Shem Tov's worldview with the cosmology of Lurianic Kabbalah? True, the Maggid of Mezhirech had transformed a poetic vision into a rigorous discipline, but he had left Baal Shem Tov's imagery intact. Rabbi Shneur Zalman was attempting something new and foreign. Seeking to create a philosophically coherent system, he would reinforce Baal Shem Tov's perceptions with the girders of Lurianic structure. Not only was the project doctrinally illegitimate, it was doomed to rob the hasidic experience of its primacy:

> I have seen *Sefer ha-Benonim* ("Book of the Middle Class") that His Honor printed and I don't see there much of use to save souls because the abundance of advice will produce a religion of rote, the learning will become a singsong. Whereas according to the way of the kabbalists, one spark is enough; it divides into several tastes, for such is the way of Torah. Too much oil douses the wick.
>
> Thus was the custom of our predecessors: They would spare their words so as not to transmit to the majority of hasidim other than words of admonishment and bring them into the covenant of belief in the righteous. A word of Torah was trim and clean. A little contained a lot. Blessing was found in that word; a hidden light would illuminate it.[39]

Rabbi Abraham of Kalisk objected to the proposed digest of hasidic counsel. True counsel of a sage could not be learned book-fashion. It had to prick one's consciousness like a blade. One word uttered by master to disciple would remain for life and grow to fruition within the depths of spirit.[40] But a collection of words?! Rather than jolt the hasid from habit, they would lull him into complacency. One rock wakes one up; continued rocking puts one to sleep.

Hasidism was a discipline, but not a system. Thus a digest of moral sayings was self-defeating. Hasidism for the masses was an oxymoron.[41]

This basic difference between HaBaD and the other branches of

Hasidism remains to this day. Other hasidic groups believe the way to God is through *emunah peshutah*, simple faith; HaBaD teaches that faith must be studied as a science. An adherent of the HaBaD way will devote time each day to furthering his understanding of hasidic belief. Rabbi Shneur Zalman responded in writing to Rabbi Abraham of Kalisk's critique by quoting the Talmud that even "a thief about to break into a home calls upon God." Faith alone without proper study will not do.[42]

Perhaps the most aggressive critic of Shneur Zalman's new way was Baal Shem Tov's grandson, Baruch of Medzibezh[43], whom we mentioned earlier. So violently opposed was he to what he viewed as the perversion of his grandfather's teaching, that his nephew, Nahman of Braslav once quipped to Shneur Zalman: "You were able to gain release from "Feterburg" (Saint Petersburg), but you won't escape so easily the wrath of "Feter Burch" (Uncle Baruch)!"[44]

Tanya itself got mixed reviews among Polish *zaddikim*. Baruch of Medzibezh's initial reaction was that it is truly an ethical manual.[45] The Seer of Lublin, Rabbi Jacob Isaac Horowitz, wrote that when he opens the *Tanya*, "vert ihm finster in die oigen" (it becomes dark for him in the eyes), which *Zemah Zedek* turned into a compliment.[46] On the other hand, Rabbi Zevi Elimelekh of Dynow emerged as a defender of the *Tanya* and its novellae, whether they be in the realm of Kabbalah[47] or Halakha.[48] Finally, closer to our own day, Rabbi Samuel Bornstein of Sochaczew, who himself developed an intellectual brand of hasidism, deeply identified with the author of the *Tanya*.[49]

The tribute paid by Rabbi Levi Isaac of Berdichev would more than compensate for the mixed reviews. Rabbi Levi Isaac, a close friend and related by marriage to Rabbi Shneur Zalman, expressed his amazement that the author had succeeded in fitting a God so vast in a book so small.[50]

In the midst of these internal hasidic differences, in 1798, Shneur Zalman was arrested and tried in Saint Petersburg for treason at the instigation of the *mitnagdim*. Shneur Zalman was released on the 19th of Kislev (the *yahrzeit* or anniversary of the death of his beloved teacher, the Maggid), just as he was reciting the words in Psalm 55:19, *Padah be-shalom nafshi*, "He liberated my soul in peace."[51] To this day, these words are sung every year at the Yud-Tet Kislev celebration.

After release from prison, Shneur Zalman transferred his residence from Liozno to Liady. In the aftermath of his harrowing experience, he circulated to the hasidim an epistle, "Katonti," in which he implored them to act humbly and not antagonize their brother Jews of the mitnagdic stripe.[52] He was free of thoughts of vengeance. At the same time, he hardened his resolve to spread his unique brand of hasidism.[53] The "Alter Rebbe" passed away at age 68, on the 24th of Tevet, 1813, fleeing Napoleon's invasion force. To Shneur Zalman's thinking, Napoleon, who would introduce the allure of Western civilization, posed a greater threat to Judaism than all the brutalities of czarist rule.

Before his death, he asked his grandson Menahem Mendel if he was able to see the ceiling. Menahem Mendel asked him what he meant by this question. Shneur Zalman explained that he could no longer see the rafters, only the word of God vivifying them.[54]

The name *Shneur*, which has been interpreted as if it were two words, *shnei or*, "two lights," is symbolic.[55] In many ways, Shneur Zalman was attempting to fuse two lights. He acted as a bridge between the *nigleh* and the *nistar*, which is to say, the exoteric and esoteric aspects of Torah. He strove to close the gap between the intellectualism of Lithuania and the mysticism of Podolia. He tried to graft Baal Shem Tov's hasidism onto Lurianic kabbalah. Finally, he acted as a conduit between Erets Israel and the Diaspora, communicating the message of the hasidic leaders in the Holy Land to their followers in Russia, while at the same time raising funds from the Jews of Russia for the upkeep of their brethren in Palestine.

The essence of the *Alter Rebbe* (Old Rabbi) was love for his Creator. Numerically, two times the word *or* (light) [207] gives the equivalent of *ve-ahavta* (You shall love) [414].[56] In Shneur Zalman's musical compositions (of which traditionally there are ten), as in his discourses, one feels the passion of his soul.[57] His longing for *En Sof*, the Infinite, takes him beyond the constriction of all the worlds; the fire burning in his breast is more than a human can sustain. It results in a state known by hasidim as *bittul bi-meziut*, "existential nullification."[58]

Menahem Mendel of Lubavitch reported that in a state of ecstasy his grandfather, Shneur Zalman uttered these words:

> I desire nothing. I don't want Your Garden of Eden, I don't want Your World to Come. All I want is You Yourself.[59]

Dov Baer Shneuri of Lubavitch and Aaron Halevi Horowitz of Staroje Selo

It was the eldest of Shneur Zalman's three sons, Dov Baer, who ascended the "throne" of the founder of HaBaD. As discussed previously, he had been groomed for this position during his father's lifetime (much to the chagrin of Rabbi Abraham of Kalisk).[60] Yet the succession was hardly smooth. Rabbi Shneur Zalman had left an eminent disciple, Aaron Halevi Horowitz of Staroje Selo who had studied with him for thirty years.[61] Evidently, in the opinion of some disciples, he was more qualified than Dov Baer to lead the group.[62] Unable to settle their differences, Aaron established his "court" in Staroje Selo, while Dov Baer maintained his center in Lubavitch. Thereafter, this White Russian town would remain the home of HaBaD hasidism into the twentieth century.

This was not merely a power struggle; there were ideological differences between the two teachers.[63] The Staroselyer emphasized ecstatic prayer; the *Mitteler Rebbe* ("Middle Rabbi")[64] cautioned against outward displays of emotion. He wrote a carefully written analysis of different forms and grades of ecstasy, *Kuntress ha-Hitpaalut*, which has been translated into English as, *A Tract on Ecstasy*. According to oral tradition, the *Alter Rebbe* would roll, so frenzied was his prayer; his son, the *Mitteler Rebbe* would stand unmoved as a stone during prayer.[65]

The Staroselyer line continued for one or two more generations, then petered out. Curiously enough, his books, which were out of print for years, enjoyed a comeback in this country at the behest of an enigmatic figure, Rabbi Hayyim Abraham Dov Baer Hakohen Levine, referred to by his small band of followers as "the *Malakh*" (Angel).[66]

As for Dov Baer, despite a weak constitution, he led a most active life, at times acting as a goodwill ambassador for HaBaD. Thus we find him unsuccessfully trying to sell the aged Talmudic genius Rabbi Akiba Eger of Posen and his younger contemporary Rabbi Mordecai Banet of Nikolsburg on the wisdom of HaBaD.[67] One of his most significant achievements was the establishment of a HaBaD center in the Biblical city of Hebron, burial site of the Patriarchs and Matriarchs. After his passing, his own daughter, Menucha Rachel and her husband Rabbi Jacob Culi (Slonim) would settle there.[68] Dov Baer also founded agricultural colonies in southern Russia (Kherson district) to improve the economic plight of Russian Jewry.

Rabbi Dov Baer passed away exactly on his fifty-fourth birthday, the ninth of Kislev, 1828. He was succeeded by Menahem Mendel, his son-in-law and nephew (son of his sister Deborah Leah). Menahem Nahum, son of Dov Baer, relates the circumstances of his father's last hour on earth.[69] Though his body was drained of life and natural heat, in what would appear to be a trancelike state, Dov Baer held forth on the kabbalistic mysteries for over an hour. When he came to the verse, *For with you is the source of Life*,[70] his soul finally expired.[71]

It may be of interest to modern (or post-modern) readers that Rabbi Dov Baer was perhaps the first to bring into sharp focus the different interests of spirituality, on the one hand, and religion, on the other, which he expresses as the dichotomy of prayer and return versus Torah and commandments.[72]

MENAHEM MENDEL SCHNEERSOHN

Rabbi Menahem Mendel inherited Rabbi Shneur Zalman's genius. Orphaned at an early age and raised in the *Alter Rebbe*'s home, he benefited from an unusually close relationship with his maternal grandfather. Until his marriage, the old man would still take his beloved grandson under his prayer shawl during the priestly benediction.

What sets the grandfather, Shneur Zalman and grandson, Menahem Mendel apart from the other members of the Schneersohn dynasty is the fact that they alone, on account of their halakhic genius and output, were embraced universally (even, begrudgingly, by *mitnagdim*, opponents of hasidism) as authorities on Jewish Law. In fact, Menahem Mendel is generally referred to as *Zemah Zedek*,[73] after the title of his collection of *halakhic* responsa.

Rabbi Menahem Mendel was as eclectic as he was prolific. (He was able to fill a page of 35 lines in 5 minutes flat,[74] and in the course of a lifetime penned 24,000 signatures,[75] or 192,000 pages!) As his grandfather before him, he was equally adept at Jewish Law, Philosophy and Kabbalah. But whereas the *Alter Rebbe* for the most part keeps the two disciplines of *halakha* (law) and *kabbalah* (mysticism) separate, his grandson attempts a fascinating fusion of the two.

Also reminiscent of Rabbi Shneur Zalman, he seems to have been interested in achieving a rapprochement with the leaders of the opposing mitnagdic tradition. In 1843, he met Rabbi Isaac of Volozhin at a rabbinic commission in St. Petersburg. (Isaac's father, Hayyim of Volozhin, was the preeminent disciple of the Vilna Gaon, Rabbi Elijah.[76]) Isaac of Volozhin was duly impressed with his hasidic counterpart's erudition and saintliness.[77] By this time, the *mitnagdim* were coming to realize the real threat to Orthodox Judaism was not from Hasidism but rather from the winds of *Haskalah* or Enlightenment blowing from the West. Menahem Mendel confided to a young *mitnagdic* rabbi under his tutelage:

> Our hasidim do not know and cannot appreciate the favor the Vilna Gaon did for us by opposing us. Were it not for the controversy, there were truly grounds to worry that the new approach would gradually lead us over the border of Torah tradition. Not unfounded was the fear that as a result of the ecstasy of the new way, that swept up its founders,

> eventually the Talmud would be burnt by the fire of the Kabbalah, the hidden Torah would obscure the revealed Torah, and the practical commandments would be reduced in value in the face of emotions seething from the mysteries of *kavvanot* (kabbalistic intentions).
>
> Even my grandfather's book, *Shulhan Arukh*, I know for a fact, was created only as an outcome of the controversy, to bring the hearts of our hasidim closer to the *halakhic* way of life, and to glorify the exoteric Torah, that they might reserve time for its serious study. If the controversy came only to produce these volumes—it would be sufficient for us! [78]

To appreciate the enormous, encyclopedic scholarship of Rabbi Menahem Mendel, one has only to compare the two volumes of his grandfather's discourses he published. The first volume, *Torah Or* (on Genesis and Exodus) is dwarfed by the sequel volume, *Likkutei Torah* (on Leviticus, Numbers and Deuteronomy). The difference in size is attributable to the fact that Rabbi Menahem Mendel packed every page of *Likkutei Torah* with copious references to the entire corpus of Judaic literature, whether it be Talmud, Midrash or Zohar.[79] Indeed, the editor was so satisfied with the final result that he comforted hasidim disappointed that the Messiah had not arrived in 1848 as expected, by saying: "Is it not enough of a revelation for you that *Likkutei Torah* was published this year?!"[80] (By the way, though certainly not the Messiah, there were significant political upheavals in Western Europe in the *annus mirabilis*, 1848.)

Zemah Zedek's fame spread far and wide. When the brilliant and enigmatic master of Polish hasidism, Menahem Mendel of Kotzk (whom Heschel has immortalized in his study, *A Passion for Truth*), passed away in 1859, some of his disciples went over to Menahem Mendel of Lubavitch. One of these disciples who combined the traditions of Polish hasidism—Kotzk and Gur—together with that of HaBaD, was Rabbi Hillel Moshe Meshel Gelbstein, who later settled in Jerusalem. In his work *Mishkenot le-Abir Yaakov*, Gelbstein records a personal prophecy made to him by the Lubavitcher which came true.[81]

EIZIK EPSTEIN OF HOMEL AND HILLEL MALISOV OF PARITCH

To think that only rebbes of the Schneersohn lineage could be considered authoritative interpreters of HaBaD tradition, would be a misconception. Two especially gifted *mashpi'im* (literally "influencers," i.e. teachers*) to rise from the ranks of the hasidim, were Rabbi Eizik Epstein of Homel [Russian, Gomel] (1780-1857) and his companion, Rabbi Hillel Malisov of Paritch [Parici] (1795-1864). Both these men spanned three generations of rebbes. Their attachment to HaBaD started during the lifetime of the *Alter Rebbe*, continued with the *Mitteler Rebbe* and peaked with *Zemah Zedek*.

"Reb Eizil Homlyer" (as he is known among hasidim) writes on the problem of intersubjectivity:

> It is called *Kabbalah* (receiving) because one must receive it from his teacher. The receiving is accomplished by the teacher drawing down to the student from the root of the student's soul . . . Truly, Maimonides, of blessed memory, was mistaken when he thought philosophical reason had brought him his immense awareness of God. Truly, it was but the power of his divine soul of an exalted niveau. Really, he was recognizing the divinity by the power of his soul."[82]

In other words, the only way to teach another human being about God, is by putting that person in touch with the divinity within his or

---

* Roughly in the year 1924, the great Polish rebbes of Gur and Sokolov made a pilgrimage to Jerusalem. The famed HaBaD *mashpi'a* Rabbi Zalman Havlin paid a visit to the Sokolover. The Sokolover asked him: "Are you the one known as 'Reb Zalman the *Mashpi'a*'?" The answer being affirmative, the Sokolover then asked, "What is a *mashpi'a*?" To which the answer came back: "We put Kabbalah in terms of *'avodah* (divine service)." The Sokolover, known for his dry wit, responded: "We also discuss Kabbalah, but we speak *deitch lashon* (i.e. Yiddish)." Cited in M. Y. Weinstock, *Shulhan ha-Ma'arakhot be-Sitrei ha-Hokhmah* III [Jerusalem, 1977], pp. 56-57.

her own soul. Similarly, Rabbi Eizik's companion, Rabbi Hillel, taught that the highest level of attainment is the revelation of the true root of one's soul as it is.[83]

JUDAH LEIB OF KOPYST; HAYYIM SHNEUR ZALMAN OF LIADY; SAMUEL OF LUBAVITCH

When Menahem Mendel passed on in 1866 at age 77, three of his six sons became *rebbes* in the HaBaD tradition. Judah Leib (MaHaRIL) founded the Kopyster school. His son, Shelomo Zalman, eldest of the rabbi's grandsons, authored the hasidic work, *Magen Avot*.[84] Shelomo Zalman of Kopyst was succeeded by his brother, Shalom Dov Baer of Retchitsa,[85] who in turn was succeeded by the youngest of the three brothers, Shemariah Noah of Bobroisk.[86] With the death of Rabbi Shemariah Noah of Bobroisk in 1926, this line came to an end. In its heyday, Kopyst counted among its hasidim some of the great talents in Russian Jewry: Joseph Rosen of Rogatchov and Dvinsk,[87] Judah Leib Zirelsohn of Kishinev, Abraham Isaac Kook,[88] Hillel Zeitlin,[89] Solomon Joseph Zevin and Nissan Telushkin.[90]

Hayyim Shneur Zalman, the third of Zemah Zedek's sons, founded the Liady school of HaBaD. In the next and, for all intents and purposes, final generation of this line,[91] Ladier hasidim were led by Rabbi Isaac Dov Baer (MaHaRID), whose prayer book with hasidic commentary was published in Berdichev on the eve of World War I.[92]

Remarkably, it was the youngest of Menahem Mendel's sons, Samuel, who inherited his rabbinate in Lubavitch. Rabbi Samuel (MaHaRaSH) lived in comfort and luxury. His wealth was legendary. It is said that his father raised him this way from youth.

An interesting anecdote relates an impromptu meeting between Rabbi Samuel and Rabbi Israel Lipkin (or Salanter, after his birthplace), dour founder of the Lithuanian Mussar or Ethical movement, whose specialty was scathing self-criticism. It seems the poor Salanter was trudging on foot along the dusty path to some European health spa, when there pulled up alongside him the royal carriage of the hasidic leader. Rabbi Samuel offered the Lithuanian rabbi a ride. Rabbi Salanter refused. Thinking the Torah scholar might have been fearful of a forbidden mixture of wool and linen in the upholstery, the Lubavitcher assured him the authority *Shevut Yaakov* permitted sitting on such seats. "Yes," retorted Rabbi Israel, "but he did not allow *gaavah* (haughtiness)."[93]

There do not appear to have been any appreciable ideological differences between the three courts. The threeway controversy which erupted between Bobroisk, Lubavitch and Liady at the turn of the twentieth century was of a strictly financial nature, concerning the equitable division of funds earmarked for Kollel HaBaD in Erets Israel.[94] For the most part, the grandchildren of Menahem Mendel continued his approach; in Kopyst and Liady, the discourses were based on his writings, of which each received a fair share. This is not to say that the cousins could not take opposite sides on any given question. At the rabbinical conference in St. Petersburg in 1910, Rabbi Shemariah Noah of Bobroisk took the side of Rabbis Meir Simcha of Dvinsk[95] and David Friedman of Karlin, who favored Russian language instruction for rabbis,[96] while his cousin, Rabbi Shalom Dov Baer of Lubavitch, together with Rabbis Hayyim Soloveichik of Brisk and Israel Meir Kagan of Radin, opposed the government's effort to impose this secular study on the rabbis.[97]

SHALOM DOV BAER SCHNEERSOHN

Though the fifth rebbe of the Schneersohn dynasty passed away well into this century, it is difficult to be objective concerning him. In the consciousness of many, the man assumes mythic proportions. There are a couple of reasons for this. First, the old men who served as the link between the original HaBaD in Russia and the attempt to recreate it in America, were to varying degrees, his disciples. Secondly when the seventh and last rebbe of Lubavitch, Menahem Mendel II spoke of the "Rebbe" without modifiers, he was referring to Rabbi Shalom Dov Baer, though he never saw him in the flesh. Thus, for many growing up in this generation in America, RaSHaB (acronym of Rabbi Shalom Baer) was the archetypal rebbe.

RaSHaB has been referred to as, "the RaMBaM (Maimonides) of hasidism." If HaBaD in general excels in being a systematic study, RaSHaB is the systematizer among systematizers. There is an order and control to his presentation which is awe-inspiring. By the same token, we know from the personal testimonies that he was an active visionary. Perhaps it is this quality, more than any other, that personifies HaBaD: the unusual ability to combine ecstasy—"holy madness" (*shetut di-kedusha*), as RaSHaB called it—and rational thought.[98]

RaSHaB was also a leader. On several occasions it was he and Rabbi Hayyim Soloveichik of Brisk (Brest-Litovsk) who together mapped out strategy for Jewish survival in Russia during the waning years of the Romanov dynasty.[99] Remarkably, these two scions of opposite traditions[100] saw eye to eye on many issues affecting the Jewish People. They were equally opposed to Zionism. In RaSHaB's "position paper" on Zionism,[101] what clinches that Herzl was inspired by the "Other Side" and not the "Side of Holiness," is the fact that he rode a horse on the Sabbath in Jerusalem, of all places. If at all he had been inspired by sanctity, his pilgrimage to the Holy City would have brought him closer to observance. The fact that Herzl's visit to the Holy Land did not net an appreciable return to religion, meant for RaSHaB that no spark of holiness was to be found in the Zionist movement.

Another negative stance taken by the two leaders of Russian Jewry, was their antagonism to the formation of Agudat Israel, a world organization of Orthodox Jewry along modern political lines.

Perhaps RaSHaB's crowning achievement was the establishment of Tomchei Temimim, the yeshiva in Lubavitch. Until its founding in 1897, Lubavitchers had no *yeshiva* or rabbinical academy to call their own. He imbued the yeshiva with the spirit of hasidism, expecting the students to excel not only in Talmud and Codes, but in DAH (acronym for *Divrei Elohim Hayyim*, "words of the Living God") as well.

It should also be mentioned that out of concern for the spiritual welfare of his Sefardic or oriental brethren in southern Russia, RaSHaB dispatched Lubavitch emissaries to the "mountain Jews" of the Caucasus.

In his final days, RaSHaB set the tone for HaBaD resistance to Communist oppression. When RaSHaB died in Rostov-on-Don on the second of Nissan, 1920, the Bolsheviks were already closing in on him. A couple of weeks earlier, agents of the regime had burst into his home during the traditional Purim celebration. RaSHaB's response was absolutely fearless.[102] It was this spirit of *mesirut nefesh* (self-sacrifice) for ideals, inherited from his holy ancestors and communicated to his only son, Joseph Isaac, that gave Lubavitchers the inner resources necessary to endure seventy years of tyrannical Soviet rule, on the one hand, and to breathe the soul of hasidism into materialist Western society, on the other.

At the very end, RaSHaB told his beloved only son, Joseph Isaac:

> *Ich geh in himmel. Die kesovim loz Ich far eich. Nehmt mich in zaal. Vellen mir zein in einem.* (I am going to heaven. The writings I leave for you. Take me into the hall [used for a synagogue]. We will be one.)

At which, Joseph Isaac was taken aback. Seeing his consternation, RaSHaB rebuked:

> Emotion (*hitpaalut*)? Emotion? Brains (*mohin*)! Brains! [103]

Moments later, the Rebbe's soul departed. From that point on, Joseph Isaac took on a new strength.

An issue common to mysticism in general is how to view "normal" non-mystical reality. Having glimpsed an alternate reality that makes greater claims of validity, should we commend to the realm of illusion the spatio-temporal coordinates our minds lock onto as we reenter Earth's orbit? In the case of halakhic Judaism, it is not just a world-picture, but the Torah, representing an entire legal system, that lends credence to this fragmented, non-unitive scheme of things. How could the religious court stone an individual for having committed an act if the guilty party's action is mere illusion? One may take this a step further. If the stoning itself is illusory, then the concept of reward and punishment becomes utterly nonsensical. Rabbi Shalom Dov Baer stated in unequivocal terms: "The world is not totally false; all that was created, exists."[104] Consciously or not, RaSHaB's formal argument for the validity of ordinary reality follows on the heels of his grandfather's subtle linguistic analysis: "*All before Him are reckoned as nought*, does not mean that they [vegetable, animal, man, stones, houses, dust, etc.—B.N] have no existence; this would be 'nought' literally, when the intention is 'as nought' in the figurative sense."[106]

JOSEPH ISAAC SCHNEERSOHN

A secularist Yiddish writer who visited Lubavitch on the eve of World War I, had the following to say concerning Joseph Isaac Schneersohn:

> As concerns the rebbe's only son, the pretender to the "throne," he is less intelligent, not a scholar and both his spiritual and moral physiognomy do not give any hope that he will be in a state to hold up the Lubavitcher kingdom with the brilliance that his father [Shalom Dov Baer], grandfather [Samuel] and great-grandfather [Menahem Mendel] ruled. The "last link" of Lubavitch is, as it appears, much strained. And we therefore have sufficient grounds to think that the present Lubavitcher Rebbe is the last, and that the light of Lubavitcher hasidism is about to go out.[107]

The journalist predicts for the Lubavitcher court the same fate that met the Kopyster and Ladier courts.

Never has a prediction been more wrong. The man who impressed his observer as being devoid of character emerged in the blackest hour of European Jewry as a giant, indomitable spirit. Neither the dungeon of Leningrad's Spalerna Prison, nor the aerial bombardment of Warsaw by the Nazi Luftwaffe could break the saint's determination to preserve the heritage of Judaism and Hasidism. Exiled from Russia, he reestablished Lubavitch hasidism in Poland; forced to flee Poland, he planted the seed of hasidism in what others viewed as the intractable soil of America.

From the time he succeeded his father in 1920, until his deportation from Russia in 1927, Schneersohn fought a valiant struggle to maintain Jewish life and institutions despite the determination of the *Yevsektsia* (Jewish Section) of the new regime to stamp them out. Finally, he was arrested and sentenced to death. Only the intervention of world Jewry on his behalf spared his life.

Some precious anecdotes emerge from those last months in Russia:

> A Russian officer held a revolver to Schneersohn's temple. The rebbe responded stoically: "When a man has many gods and but one world, he fears the 'toy.' I, who have but one God and many worlds, am not afraid."[108]

> At the station, as he was about to board the train to the West, leaving behind his beloved hasidim (many of whom would suffer torture and be sentenced to labor camps in what Solzhenitsyn has termed the "Gulag Archipelago"), he imparted his farewell message: "Only our bodies were delivered to exile, but not our souls."

His first destination was Riga, Latvia. In 1928, he visited Erets Israel and the United States, everywhere rekindling the spark in the souls of the hasidim. Returning to Europe, he went on to found a Lubavitch yeshiva in Otwock, a suburb of Warsaw. With the Nazi invasion of Poland, he was forced to flee to the United States, arriving in 1940. He settled in the Crown Heights area of Brooklyn. During World War II, he published a journal entitled, *Ha-Keriah ve-ha-Kedusha*, in which he called upon Jews to repent. In one issue he accurately predicted the demise of Mussolini. In his final years, up to his passing on the tenth of Shevat, 1950, he showed superhuman strength in his resolve to spread Judaism to all corners of the globe, whether it be the establishment of a religious day school in New Haven, setting up a hasidic village in Erets Israel, or dispatching emissaries to Morocco.

Joseph Isaac is remembered by those who knew him intimately, not as an intellectual, but as an incomparable *baal mesirut nefesh*, "master of self-sacrifice," and as a *baal hergesh*, an emotional person.

At the end of his days, he was confined to a wheelchair. When his attendant strapped on him the phylacteries (the rebbe unable to "lay" the *tefillin* without assistance), Joseph Isaac remarked:

Va'ani tefillati. Dos bin Ich. (This is what I am. I am a prayer.)

MENAHEM MENDEL SCHNEERSON (II)

There would seem to be a pattern in the Schneerson dynasty, whereby the propensity for intellectualism skips a generation. The founder of the dynasty, Shneur Zalman; his grandson, Menahem Mendel;[109] his grandson, Shalom Dov Baer; and finally his grandson-in-law, Menahem Mendel II, stand out as the geniuses of this lineage.

So much has already been written concerning this outstanding individual, that one feels at a loss to record any more than a skeletal biography of Rabbi Menahem Mendel Schneerson. He was born 1902 in Nikolayev, a patrilineal descendant of Menahem Mendel I, the *Zemah Zedek*, through his eldest son, Baruch Shalom. His father, Levi Isaac, a kabbalist of note, served as rabbi of Yekatrinoslav (later renamed "Dnepropetrovsk" by the Bolsheviks), until he was sentenced to years of exile for his Jewish activities. As the fiance of Rabbi Joseph Isaac's second daughter, Haya Mushka, Menahem Mendel left Russia with the Rebbe's entourage in 1927. It was not the young man's plan to ever become *rebbe*. Instead, he studied in university in Berlin and later at the Sorbonne in Paris, receiving a degree in engineering.[110]

Schneerson and his wife escaped from occupied France to the United States in 1941. At first, he worked for the U.S. government in the Brooklyn Navy Yard. Through all this period, up until his father-in-law's passing in 1950, he studiously avoided the limelight, preferring a private existence. From time to time, he did assist in his father-in-law's activities, but in general, his profile was such that many naturally assumed that when the day came, it would be the Rebbe's first son-in-law, Rabbi Shemaryah Gurary (RaSHaG), married to his eldest daughter, Hannah, who would succeed as *rebbe*.

Again, history is full of surprises. The mild-mannered Menahem Mendel Schneerson, soft-spoken and courtly, proved to be a "superman." Under his leadership, Lubavitch became the empire it is today, "upon which the sun never sets" (to borrow an old British slogan). He was equally adept at Talmud as at Kabbalah, besides being a brilliant mathematician and gifted linguist. Rabbi Schneerson may have downplayed the mystical side of hasidism in order to stress the practical observance of Judaism *be-po'al mamash* (in action). This would conform to the role his predecessors foresaw for the Messiah. The *Mitteler Rebbe*, Rabbi Dov Baer, for example, wrote that the "crown of a good name"[111] of Messiah is formed of our actual observance of commandments, not from mystical *kavvanot* (intentions).[112]

This last rebbe of Lubavitch excelled at statesmanship and manipulation of modern media. He could make or break an Israeli government. The denizen of the spiritual world was so successful in the temporal realm, that many of his followers were convinced he was the long-awaited King Messiah.[113] As he and his wife were childless, in terms of succession, this meant "the end of the line." Haya Mushka passed on in 1988. The *histalkut* (passing) of Rabbi Menahem Mendel in 1994, has thrown Lubavitcher hasidism into a state of turmoil such as the movement has never known in over two hundred years of its existence. What will be the future of this movement, only the One above knows.

FOOTNOTES

1. Most revealing in this regard is the letter of Rabbi Eizik Epstein of Homel published at the conclusion of his *Hanah Ariel*, III (Berdichev: Sheftel, 1912). Epstein writes that all hasidim believe "*Altz iz Gott*" (All is God), even the world preceived as darkness. Among the Chernobyl hasidim the belief takes on a wilder form, whereas among the HaBaD hasidim the belief is more refined. This in contradistinction to the *mitnagdim*, among whom the belief is quite dormant. Epstein's process of "reeducation" began under Shneur Zalman's tutelage. In the writer's own words: "I vomited my mother's milk over this belief." His process was completed under the personal guidance of the Rebbe's son, Dov Baer. By the time the latter had finished speaking, "he had shot into me an arrow of light and strong belief, to the point there was aroused in me a desire to go and scream all this in the streets."

2. Cited in Shneur Zalman of Liady, *Tanya*, II, chapter 1, (p. 76b).

3. Ibid. See also *Tanya* IV, chapter 25, (p. 139a).

4. The Polish spelling is "Miedzyboz." The Yiddish pronunciation is "Mezbizh." Mezbizh's claim to fame was that a century earlier Rabbi Joel Sirkes, author of *Bayit Hadash* (BaH), served there as rabbi. See J. L. Maimon, *Sarei ha-Me'ah*, III (Jerusalem: Mossad Harav Kook, 1950), pp. 11-19.

5. Dan Ben-Amos and Jerome R. Mintz trans. and ed., *In Praise of the Baal Shem Tov* [*Shivhei ha-Besht*] (Northvale, NJ: Jason Aronson, 1993), pp. 106-107.

6. Jacob Joseph of Polonnoye, *Ben Porat Yosef* (Piotrkow, 1884; photo offset New York, 1954), 27c.

7. Ibid., 85b.

8. Saadia Gaon, *The Book of Beliefs and Opinions*, translated from the Arabic and the Hebrew by Samuel Rosenblatt (New Haven: Yale University Press, 1976) 10:7.

9. Eliezer Zevi Hakohen Zweifel, *Shalom 'al Yisrael* (Zitomir, 1868; facs. ed. Jerusalem: Makor, 1970), pp. 57-59. See also Gershom Scholem, *Devarim be-Go* (Tel Aviv: Am Oved, 1976), p. 321.

10. The derivative version of *Keter Shem Tov* reads: "It is worthy for a man to learn from the desire of material things how to desire the service of God and His love" (*Keter Shem Tov* [Kehot: Brooklyn, 1972], 9a, par. 64). The

verb "to learn" truly suggests a cognitive process, as gathered by Zweifel, but that verb is lacking altogether in the original. *Keter Shem Tov* by Aaron ben Zevi Hirsch Hakohen of Apta, is an early collection of teachings of Baal Shem Tov extracted from the works of Jacob Joseph Hakohen of Polonnoye. It was first published in Zolkiew in 1794.

11. M. Piekarz, *The Beginnings of Hasidism/Ideological Trends* in *Derush and Mussar Literature* (Jerusalem: Bialik Institute, 1978), pp. 207-208.

12. Cited in Elijah de Vidas, *Reshit Hokhmah, Shaar ha-ahavah*, chap. 4. Rabbi Isaac of Acre narrates a lengthy tale of a commoner who falls in love with a princess and eventually ends up a holy man: " . . . As a result of his separation from everything sensate by connecting his thought constantly to one object, and his concentration and his total desire, his soul was divested of the sensible forms and returned to cleave to the intelligibles. His soul was divested of everything sensate, even of the woman, and clung to God, until within a short time . . . he became a perfect servant, a holy man of God." In those Tales of the Ascetics (*maasiyot ha-perushim*),Isaac of Acre adds the Sufi saying, "He who has not desired a woman is like a donkey and even less!" Cf. the Turkish Sufi anecdote concerning Sheikh Jemal Halveti in *Love is the Wine* (Putney, Vermont: Threshold Books, 1987), p. 10. In Talmudic tradition, the donkey is seen as a cold-natured animal. See Talmud Bavli, *Shabbat* 53a; Simon ben Zemah Duran, *Magen Avot* (Livorno 1785; facsimile ed. Jerusalem: Makor Publishing Ltd., N.D.), 67b; Reuben Margaliot, *Nefesh Hayyah, Orah Hayyim* 536:3. See further Paul B. Fenton, *Deux Traites de Mystique Juive* (Paris: Verdier, 1987), p. 104, n. 218; Moshe Idel, *Hasidism: Between Ecstasy and Magic* (Albany: State University of New York Press, 1995), pp. 18, 61-64.

Perhaps Rabbi Nahman of Braslav's tale of The Lost Princess should be correlated to Rabbi Isaac of Acre's tale:

> She said, " . . . Choose yourself a place and remain there for an entire year. All that year you must long to get me out. Whenever you are unoccupied you must only yearn, seek and look forward to freeing me" (Aryeh Kaplan trans., *Rabbi Nachman's Stories* [Brooklyn and Jerusalem: Breslov Research Institute, 1983], p. 40).

13. David Cohen, *Kol ha-Nevuah* (Jerusalem: Mossad Harav Kook, 1979), p. 124. In addition to the passage in *Beliefs and Opinions*, Cohen adduced a

parallel in Saadyah's *Commentary to Sefer Yezirah* as cited in Judah ben Barzilai of Barcelona's *Commentary to Sefer Yezirah*. However I would be surprised to learn that Baal Shem Tov had access to either work. Both commentaries remained in manuscript until fairly recently. Judah ben Barzilai of Barcelona's commentary was published by S. Z. H. Halberstamm in 1885 and Saadyah's by M. Lambert in 1891.

Cohen (ibid.) also juxtaposes the anonymous medieval *Shir ha-Yihud* (*Hymn of Divine Unity*), which contains some of the boldest immanentist imagery in all Judaic literature, and was assumed by many to reflect Saadyah's theology. This assertion, first evidenced in Moses of Tachau's thirteenth century work *Ketav Tamim* (facsimile edition of Paris, Bibliotheque Nationale, ms. H711, Jerusalem: Akademon, 1984) later surfaces on the frontispiece to the Thiengen 1560 edition of the *Hymn* (numbered facsimile edition, Jerusalem: Jewish National and University Press, 1981). But it is just as likely Baal Shem Tov would have contented himself with the traditional ascription of *Shir ha-Yihud* to Rabbi Samuel, father of Rabbi Judah the Hasid of Regensburg or to Rabbi Judah himself. Cf. Hayyim of Volozhin, *Nefesh ha-Hayyim*, III, chap. 4. Also, as Cohen is aware (see *Kol ha-Nevuah*, p. 143, n. 18), the relation of *Shir ha-Yihud* to authentic Saadyana (as opposed to anonymous paraphrastic translation of Saadyah), is problematic. See Abraham Berliner, *Ketavim Nivharim*, I (Jerusalem: Mossad Harav Kook, 1969), pp. 148-170; Joseph Dan, *Gershom Scholem and the Mystical Dimension of Jewish History* (New York: New York University Press, 1987), pp. 103-104; Gershom G. Scholem, *Major Trends in Jewish Mysticism* (New York: Schocken Books, 1971), pp. 108-109; Isaac Baer, *Seder Avodat Israel* (Rodelheim, 1868), pp. 133, 139-140.

[Parenthetically, it is interesting to observe that both the earlier Hasidism (from Hebrew *hasid*, pious man) of medieval Germany and the later Eastern European Hasidism of Baal Shem Tov were infused with Saadyah's immanentist theology. Regarding the influence Saadyah exerted on the German mystics, see Scholem, *Major Trends*, pp. 107-109.]

Finally, Cohen (*Kol ha-Nevuah*, p. 126, n. 157) detects a trace of Saadya's terminology, taken from *Beliefs and Opinions* (Kapah ed., Arabic and Hebrew [Jerusalem, 1993], p. 80), in *Zavaat ha-RIVaSH*, an early collection of

Baal Shem Tov's sayings, but the slice of verbiage is too thin to be convincing.

14. Saadia Gaon, *Beliefs and Opinions* (Rosenblatt translation), pp. 131-132.

15. Eliezer Zevi Hakohen Zweifel, *Shalom 'al Yisrael* (Vilna: Romm, 1873), pp. 62-64; Abraham Isaac Kook, *Ikvey ha-Zon* (Jerusalem: Mossad Harav Kook, 1985), pp. 133-134; unexpurgated version publicized by Rivkah Schatz-Uffenheimer in *Yovel Orot*, ed. B. Ish Shalom (Jerusalem: World Zionist Organization, 1985), pp. 353-354; A. I. Kook, *Orot ha-Kodesh* (Jerusalem: Mossad Harav Kook, 1971), II, p. 399; Martin Buber, *The Origin and Meaning of Hasidism* (New York: Horizon Press, 1960), pp. 90-99.

See further Bezalel Naor, "Plumbing Rav Kook's Panentheism," in Moshe Sokol ed., *Engaging Modernity: Rabbinic Leaders and the Challenge of the Twentieth Century* (Northvale, NJ: Jason Aronson, 1997), pp. 86-88, n. 22.

16. *Tanya*, I, chap. 41 (p. 56a). The citation is from *Zohar, Raya Mehemna*, III, p. 225a. Cf. *Tikkunei Zohar* (Reuben Margaliot, ed.), Introduction, pp. 5a and 6b.

17. See David Cohen, *Kol ha-Nevuah*, p. 123 and the similar findings of Scholem, *Kabbalah* (New York: Meridian, 1974), pp.144-152, especially p. 147. Also Hillel Zeitlin, "Kadmut ha-mistorin be-yisrael," *Ha-Tekufah* IV (1920), p. 315, n. 1.

18. The great hasidic sage Rabbi Zadok Hakohen of Lublin laid the groundwork for this kind of examination of parallel civilizations. See his *Peri Zaddik*, I (Lublin, 1901), 69a; IV (Lublin, 1934), 8c; idem., *Resisei Laylah* (Lublin, 1903). Cited in Bezalel Naor, *Lights of Prophecy* (New York: Orthodox Union, 1990), pp. 24-25.

19. See Rabbi Nathan Sternharz of Nemirov, *Sihot ha-Ran* (B'nai Berak, 1976), p. 80, par. 117. Available in English translation: Aryeh Kaplan, *Rabbi Nachman's Wisdom* (Brooklyn, 1976), p. 245.

20. David Cohen, *Kol ha-Nevuah*, p. 125, was able to trace this *gematria* (numerical equivalence) as far back as Joseph Gikatilia's *Ginat Egoz*, composed in 1274. See *Ginat Egoz* (Jerusalem: Yeshivat Ha-Hayyim ve-ha-Shalom, 1989), p. 32. See also *Tanya*, II, chap. 6 (80a).

21. Dan Ben-Amos and Jerome R. Mintz trans. and ed., *In Praise of the Baal Shem Tov*, pp. 12-13.

22. According to Gershom Scholem, though the form "Baal Shem Tov" is

certainly rarer than "Baal Shem" (Master of the Name), the title usually given miracle workers who made theurgic use of the divine name, there were other Baal Shem Tovs besides the founder of modern hasidism: Elhanan Baal Shem Tov, Joel Baal Shem I, et al. See Scholem, *Kabbalah* (New York: Meridian, 1978), p. 311. See also the frontispieces to Elijah Baal Shem Tov, *Toldot Adam* (Kisvarda=Kleinwardein) and Wolf Baer Schiff of Zamosc, *Minhat Zikaron* (Crakow, 1894), reproduced in Moshe Hillel, *Baalei Shem* (Jerusalem: Makhon Bnai Issachar, 1993), pp. 145, 165.

In Polish tax records of the period, recently discovered in the Crakow archives of the Czartoryski family, our protagonist is referred to as "Balsem," "Balsam" or "Balszam Doktor." See Moshe Rosman, *Founder of Hasidism* (Berkeley: University of California Press, 1996), p. 165 and facsimile facing p. 1.

23. Rabbi Isaac Judah Jehiel Safrin, *Megillat Setarim*, ed. Naftali Ben-Menahem (Jerusalem: Mossad Harav Kook, 1944), pp. 32-33. The author was told the story by his uncle and teacher, Rabbi Zevi Hirsch Eichenstein of Zydaczow.

24. Dov Ben-Amos and Jerome R. Mintz, *In Praise of the Baal Shem Tov* , p. 257.

25. "Martin Buber's Interpretation of Hasidism," in *Gershom Scholem, The Messianic Idea in Judaism* (New York: Schocken, 1995), pp. 228-250. See further Joseph Dan, *Gershom Scholem and the Mystical Dimension of Jewish History* (New York: New York University Press, 1987), pp. 317-319; Laurence J. Silberstein, *Martin Buber's Social and Religious Thought* (New York: New York University Press, 1989), pp. 4-5, 13-14, 53-70; Steven T. Katz, *Post-Holocaust Dialogues* (New York: New York University Press, 1983), pp. 52-93; Moshe Idel, *Hasidism: Between Ecstasy and Magic* (Albany: State University of New York Press, 1995), pp. 2-9; Barry J. Hammer, "Resolving the Buber-Scholem Controversy in Hasidism," *Journal of Jewish Studies* (Oxford) XLVII (1996): 1, pp. 102-127.

26. Cf. remarks of Rabbi Judah Leib Hakohen Maimon, *Sarei ha-Me'ah*, III (Jerusalem: Mossad Harav Kook, 1950), pp. 19-20. Also Introduction to Rabbi Shlomo Joseph Zevin, *Sippurei Hasidim/Mo'adim* (Jerusalem: Beit Hillel, n.d.) on behalf of the HaBaD tradition and Zevin's own comparison of teachings and tales to *Halakha* and *Aggadah* (ibid., p. 5).

27. Zwi Batscha, *Salomon Maimon's Lebensgeschichte* (Frankfurt am Main:

Insel Verlag, 1984), pp. 116-117.

28. Solomon Maimon, *An Autobiography*, tr. J.C. Murray (1888), ed. Moses Hadas (New York: Schocken Books, 1947), p. 54.

29. Wolf Zeev Rabinowitsch, *Lithuanian Hasidism* (New York: Schocken Books, 1971), p. xi.

30. See Raphael Mahler, *Hasidism and the Jewish Enlightenment* (Philadelphia: Jewish Publication Society of America, 1985).

31. One is reminded of Israeli poet Shin Shalom's line: "I am a son of those unifiers, those Jews of the flame (*lehavah*)." S. Shalom, *Yalkut Shirim* (Tel Aviv: Yavneh, 1973), p. 83. Shin Shalom, pseudonym of Shalom Shapiro, was a scion of a hasidic dynasty.

32. Simon Rawidowicz, *The Writings of Nachman Krochmal* [Hebrew] (London: Ararat Publishing Society, 1961), pp. 416-417.

33. "Introduction by author's sons" to Rabbi Shneur Zalman's *Shulhan 'Arukh* (Brooklyn: Kehot, 5751/1991), unpaginated.

34. Ibid.

35. Hayyim Meir Heilman, *Beit Rabbi* (Berdichev: Sheftel, 1902), Vol. I, p. 10 (5b in Hebrew pagination).

36. The story goes that originally Shneur Zalman had intended to publish a *Sefer shel Zaddikim* (Book of the Righteous), but the manuscript was destroyed in a fire, as had been predicted by the author's friend, the "Grandfather" of Shpole (*Shpoler Zeide*).

37. See Rabbi Shneur Zalman, "Introduction" to *Tanya*.

38. Transcribed from the copy in the collection of Nahum Dov Baer Friedman of Sadigora and annotated by Naftali Ben-Menahem, "Manuscripts from the Library of Rabbi Nahum Dov-Ber Friedman," *Areshet* (Jerusalem: Mossad Harav Kook, 1958), I:408. The editor dates the letter 1797. This letter and others which were preserved in manuscript (by the rebbe of Slonim and the rabbi of the Old City of Jerusalem) and never published, substantiate the ideological (as opposed to purely financial) basis of the falling out of Rabbi Abraham of Kalisk and Rabbi Shneur Zalman of Liady. See Rivka Schatz, "Anti-spiritualism ba-hasidut" (*Iyyunim be-torat Shneur Zalman mi-Liady*), *Molad*, 2:171-172 (November 1962), pp. 514-515.

See also *Tanya, Iggeret ha-Kodesh*, chap. 25, where Shneur Zalman justifies his attempt to explain Baal Shem Tov's teaching against the theoretical backdrop of Luria's kabbalah.

In academic circles of late, there is a tendency to call into question the authenticity of the letters of Rabbi Abraham of Kalisk, at least in the form they have come down to us. The circle of Rabbi Dov Baer Shneuri ("Mitteler Rebbe") are suspected of having doctored the letters. See Raya Haran, "Belil igrot," *Zion* 56(1991):299-320; idem, "Shivhei ha-Rav: li-she'elat aminutan shel igrot hasidim me-Erets Israel," *Katedra* 55(1990):22-58; 64 (1992):98-102; Moshe Rosman, *Founder of Hasidism* (Berkeley: University of California Press, 1996), p. 204.

39. Naftali Ben-Menahem, "Manuscripts from the Library of Rabbi Nahum Dov-Ber Friedman," pp. 408-409.

40. One notes in this regard that the early teachings of Shneur Zalman, still under the spell of the Maggid, are remarkably terse. Concerning these first short sayings, see J. I. Schneersohn, *Sefer ha-Sihot 5701* (Brooklyn: Kehot, 1964), pp. 26, 66, 100, 126, 144; Roman A. Foxbrunner, *Habad* (Northvale, NJ: Jason Aronson, 1993), p. 49.

41. Naftali Ben-Menahem, p. 409.

42. The letter is excerpted in Heilman, *Beit Rabbi*, I, pp. 84-85 [Heb. pagination 42b-43a]. Further defense of the HaBaD way may be found there on pp. 87-89 [44a-45a].

43. Baruch did not join the fray until 1802. See Shneur Zalman's letter in *RaMaH Otiyot* (limited edition, New York, 1991), pp. 36-37, par. 150. [*RaMaH Otiyot* for the most part, is a collection of anecdotal material heard from Rabbi Samuel Grunem Esterman, *mashpi'a* in Lubavitch from 1905 until the First World War.] Part of the letter appears in *Beit Rabbi*, I, p. 86 [Heb. pagination 43b].

44. H. M. Heilman, *Beit Rabbi* I, p. 131 [Hebrew pagination 66a], n. 2.

45. Letter of Shneur Zalman cited above note 43. The version of *RaMaH Otiyot* reads *mussar haskel* (ethics) while that of *Beit Rabbi* reads *sefer haskel* (intellect).

46. *RaMaH Otiyot*, p. 13, par. 59. See also *Beit Rabbi*, I, p. 87 [Heb. pagination 44a].

47. Zevi Elimelekh of Dynow, *Igra de-Pirka* (Munkacs, 1894), p. 22a (par.

132). In his gloss (no. 96) to his teacher Rabbi Zevi Hirsch Eichenstein of Zydaczow's *Hakdamah ve-Derekh le-Etz Hayyim*, alternatively titled *Sur me-Ra va-Asseh Tov*, Rabbi Zevi Elimelekh takes exception to the author's onslaught against those who would translate Luria's cosmologic kabbalah to psychology. Rabbi Zevi Elimelekh holds up as a legitimate example of such translation, Cordovero's slim volume *Tomer Deborah*. See *Sur me-Ra va-Asseh Tov* complete with RZE's glosses (Tel Aviv, 1969), 85a-86a. Isaiah Tishby (*Kiryat Sefer*, 45(1970):153, n. 127) questioned whether Eichenstein's polemic was restricted to *Tanya* alone or included as well the works of Rabbi Moses Hayyim Luzzatto. (For that matter, one could extend the polemic to Abraham Herrera, author of *Puerta del Cielo* (Hebrew, *Shaar ha-Shamayim*) and *Beit Elohim*. See David Cohen, *Kol ha-Nevuah* (Jerusalem: Mossad Harav Kook, 1970), p. 218, who contrasts *Sur me-Ra* to Joseph Ergas' *Shomer Emunim*. The latter was informed by Herrera's work.) On the basis of a later passage in *Sur me-Ra* (120a) where Eichenstein expesses his contumely of *Shaar ha-Yihud* (second part of Tanya), one is inclined to interpret the earlier passage as well as directed against *Tanya*. However, that reading is made difficult by Eichenstein's concluding exhortation commending the reader to the teachings of "Rabbi Dov Baer (of Mezhirech) and his colleagues"—hardly an appropriate conclusion to a diatribe against *Tanya*! Dov Schwarz's (*Sinai* 102:250-251, n. 51) query whether *Shaar ha-Yihud* refers to Shneur Zalman's work or to those by his son Dov Baer and disciple Aaron Halevi Horowitz of Staroje Selo (all titled *Shaar ha-Yihud*!), does not ease the difficulty, as these too are within the tradition of Rabbi Dov Baer of Mezhirech.

Tishby (ibid.) documented that Eichenstein's nephew and disciple, Rabbi Isaac Judah Yehiel Safrin of Komarno pilloried Luzzatto's kabbalistic work *Hoker u-Mekubbal* (see Safrin, *Heikhal ha-Berakha* [Lemberg, 1866], *Va-Ethanan*, 27d). In response to Tishby's article, Rabbi Hayyim Liberman, the renowned HaBaD researcher, showed that unlike the rabbi of Komarno, Rabbi Menahem Mendel of Lubavitch (*Zemah Zedek*) held Luzzatto's *Hoker u-Mekubbal* in high regard, citing from it as an important work on Kabbalah, if at times only to differ with Luzzatto's positions. See H. Liberman, *Ohel RaHeL* (New York, 1980), Vol. I, p. 74; Menahem Mendel Schneersohn, *Or ha-Torah*, *Yitro*, p. 841 and *Megillat Esther*, pp. 2426-2427.

Rabbi Zevi Elimelekh of Dinow sings the praise of *Tanya* in gloss 147 to *Sur me-Ra* (p. 121). See also Rabbi Zevi Elimelekh's *Igra de-Kallah, Mishpatim* and *B'nai Issachar, Ma'amrei Hodshei Kislev-Tevet* 3:46.

48. *Igra de-Pirka*, 35b (par. 187).

49. Joshua Uziel Zilberberg, *Malkhut Beit David* (Bnai Berak: Makhon Zekher Naftali, 1991), p. 108.

50. Heilman, *Beit Rabbi*, I, chapter 25.

51. Letters of Shneur Zalman to Levi Isaac of Berdichev and Baruch of Medzibezh. See *Beit Rabbi*, p. 70 (35b in Hebrew pagination). See also Mordecai Wilensky, *Hasidim and Mitnaggedim* [Hebrew] (Jerusalem: Bialik Institute, 1970), Vol. I, pp. 303-304.

52. Published posthumously in *Tanya*, IV, chap. 2. Even more explicit in this regard is the letter in *Beit Rabbi*, I, pp. 70-71 [Heb. pagination 35b-36a].

53. Rabbi S. B. Schneersohn observed that the discourses written after the *Alter Rebbe*'s release from Peterburg are garbed in intellect and thus geared to a wider audience. See *Torat Shalom/Sefer ha-Sihot* (Brooklyn: Kehot, 1992), pp. 112, 114. According to another descendant, Shelomo Zalman of Kopyst, "throughout the period of Liozno and at the beginning of Liady, the main service of hasidism involved the heart too; at the end of Liady, the main service was restricted to the mind" (Epistle of Shelomo Zalman to the hasidim after the death of his father, Judah Leib of Kopyst; published at beginning of *Magen Avot* [Berdichev, 1902]). The Kopyster paints there a dismal picture of a movement in decline.

Bichovsky too discusses the difference between Liozno and Liady. Shneur Zalman remarked: "Before in Liozno, when a man would come to me, he would be consumed by fire and transformed into another man. This aroused in heaven an accusation, as it would have destroyed free will. In Peterburg it was decreed above to hide away this aproach. Nevertheless, even after Peterburg, it remains the case that whoever grasps my door handle will not die without repentance" (*Kitvei ha-RHE Bichovski* [Brooklyn,1990], pp. 53-54). Yet another descendant, Rabbi Shemariah Noah of Bobroisk (younger brother of Shelomo Zalman of Kopyst), commenting on the epistle *Katonti*, pointed out another shift in terms of leadership: Before Peterburg, the *Rebbe* was in a high state, three thousand hasidim would spend the Sabbath with him and the discourses were of a very exalted nature; after Peterburg, fewer hasidim travelled to the *Rebbe* and the talks were geared to the level of the audience, yet it is those discourses that have remained (ibid., p. 150).

54. Hayyim Meir Perlov, *Likkutey Sippurim* (Kefar Habad, 1966), p. 77.

55. Menahem Mendel of Lubavitch (*Zemah Zedek*) in his letter concerning the publication of *Torah Or*. Cited in publisher's introduction to *Derekh Mizvotekha* (Poltava, 1911). Cf. *Beit Rabbi*, I, p. 126 [Heb. pagination 63b], n.10 citing Rabbi Menahem Nahum of Chernobyl. See also introduction of Menahem Nahum to his father Rabbi Dov Baer Shneuri's *Torat Hayyim* (Brooklyn: Kehot, 1993), p. vii. See Y. L. Bialer's poem, "Or ba-or nimzag." Published in the anthology *Emunim*, Pinhas Peli, ed. (Jerusalem: Mosad Harav Kook, 1954), p. 84.

56. Ibid. This *gematria* (numerical equivalence) first occurs in Hayyim Vital, *Shaar ha-Kavvanot, kavvanat keri'at shema*; idem, *Peri 'Ez Hayyim, Shaar Keri'at Shema*, chaps. 23, 25. It is cited by Rabbi Shneur Zalman. See e.g. *Tanya*, I, 43 (62b); *Torah Or, Mikkez*, 32c.

57. Shmuel Zalmanov, *Sefer ha-Niggunim* (Brooklyn: Nichoach, 1948), pp. 19, 43.

58. See Bezalel Naor, "The Song of Songs, Abulafia and the Alter Rebbe," *Jewish Review*, April-May 1990, pp. 10-11; idem., "*Hotam bolet ve-hotam shoke'a* (Raised Seal and Sunken Seal) in the Teaching of Rabbi Abraham Abulafia and the Doctrine of HaBaD," [Hebrew], *Sinai* 107 (1991), pp. 54-57.

59. *Derekh Mizvotekha, shoresh mizvat ha-tefillah*, chap. 40.

60. See Naftali Ben-Menahem, "Manuscripts from the Library of Rabbi Nahum Dov-Ber Friedman," p. 410.

61. From frontispiece to Horowitz's work, *Shaarei ha-Yihud ve-ha-Emunah* (Shklov, 1820).

62. On the other hand, Menahem Mendel of Lubavitch, who succeeded Dov Baer, once commented to his son Judah Leib, that the difference between his father-in-law's teaching and that of Aaron of Staroje Selo, was that Dov Baer counted the *Alter Rebbe*'s words like pearls, whereas the Staroselyer contented himself with the *Alter Rebbe*'s gist. See *RaMaH Otiyot*, p. 27, par. 129.

63. See Bezalel Naor, "*'Avodat Hashem be-Torat HaBaD*" (Review of Rachel Elior's *The Theory of Divinity of Hasidut Habad* [Hebrew]), *Ha-Zofeh*, 24 Tevet, 5744 (30.12.83), p. 7.

64. According to Rabbi J. I. Schneersohn, neither Eizik of Homel nor Hillel of Paritch (mid nineteenth century) employed the term "Middle Rabbi." One questions its origins. See J. I. Schneersohn, *Sefer ha-Sihot* 5701, p. 41.

65. Ibid., p. 41, par. 166 and *Beit Rabbi*, I, pp. 178-179 [Heb. pagination 89b-90a]; II, p. 184 [Heb. pagination 92b]. According to an anecdote, Shneur Zalman once told Levi Isaac of Berdichev to observe his son's behavior during prayer. Levi Isaac, who was renowned for his ecstasy, was disappointed to see that narry a tremor passed through Dov Baer's body. Only when Shneur Zalman told him to look once again, did Levi Isaac notice the young man's clothing was drenched with perspiration.

Similarly, *Zemah Zedek* compared his father-in-law's state of *bittul* (self-annihilation) to the slow burn of a wet straw of hay. The hay retains its form, but if you give it a tap, it crumbles to ash. See Shalom Dov Baer Schneersohn, *Sefer ha-Maamarim 5666* (Brooklyn: Kehot, 1991), p. 582.

66. See the memorial to Rabbi Jacob Schorr at the beginning of the folio edition of Aaron Halevi Horowitz's *Shaarei ha-Yihud ve-ha-Emunah*, 7th edition (Jerusalem, 1966).

For details concerning the *Malakh*, see Jerome R. Mintz, *Hasidic People* (Cambridge, Mass.: Harvard University Press, 1992), pp. 21-26. I have been able to piece together a few more details. Hayyim Abraham Dov Baer Hakohen Levine hailed from the town of Ilya, White Russia. A former neighbor describes the man Ilya's inhabitants referred to as "the *Malakh*":

". . . a handsome man with a magnificent long beard interlaced with silver-gray hair. A rare, interesting appearance that shone from spiritual and physical harmony—truly like an angel. He wore a long, black, broad, neat coat with a fur collar. In one hand he held a walking stick and under the other arm, the *tallit* and *tefillin*." Cited in *Sefer Ilya*, ed. A. Koppelowitz (Kefar Habad: Iggud Yoz'ei Ilya be-Yisrael, 1962), p. 294.

Levine's family's attachment to Lubavitch started in the days of the *Mitteler Rebbe*, Rabbi Dov Baer. His teacher had been Rabbi Ziskind, son of the famed Rabbi Zalman of Kurenets, a major disciple of Rabbi Shneur Zalman, founder of HaBaD. Levine's Talmudic standing made him a close confidant of the famous scholars of the generation, Rabbis Hayyim Soloveichik of Brisk and Hayyim Ozer Grodzenski of Vilna. The Rebbe of Lubavitch, Shalom Dov Baer (known as RaSHaB) engaged Levine to serve as private tutor to his only son,

Joseph Isaac. The story goes that once the tutor caught his charge reading a newspaper, a concession to modernity and worldliness the Angel could hardly tolerate. This planted the seed of a deep rift between Levine and the official leadership of Lubavitch. (There is a cryptic reference to "Abraham Dov Levine of Kurenets" in Rabbi J. I. Schneersohn's 1902 memoir published as the introduction to S. B. Schneersohn, *Kuntress u-Ma'ayan* [Brooklyn: Kehot, 1958], pp. 15-16.) Eventually the Malakh emigrated to New York, where he was able to mesmerize a contingent of students from Yeshiva Torah Va-Daat in the Williamsburg section of Brooklyn. (The Malakh himself was rabbi of a congregation in the Bronx.) Back in the thirties, it was unheard of for even the most right-wing yeshiva students to eschew secular subjects, ballplaying and western apparel. Yet the Malakh was able to convince his devotees to restrict themselves to East European garb and sacred texts. Mr. Mendlowitz, their principal, who had originally brought the students to Rabbi Levine for instruction in *Tanya*, was now forced to expel the young men from the yeshiva. (See the responsum of Rabbi Joshua Baumel to Shraga Feivel Mendlowitz permitting the expulsion, in Baumel's *Emek Halakha* [Jerusalem, 1976], II, chap. 28, pp. 272b-275b.) They set up their own *beit midrash* (house of study), Netivot Olam, which continues in Williamsburg to this day. (Ironically, into the next generation, the leader of the Malakhim was Rabbi Jacob Schorr, while his brother Gedaliah, who remained in the yeshiva, went on to become the dean of Torah Va-Daat.) Another center of Malakhim, as they are known, flourishes in Monsey, an upstate suburb of New York City. There they continue what they view as the authentic tradition of HaBaD, uncontaminated by the trappings of Western Civilization, be they secular knowledge, stylish dress or the modern State of Israel. The "Malakh" passed away on the first day of Shavuot, 1938. A collection of his letters has been published under the title, *Ozar Igrot Kodesh*.

It seems the Malakh also impressed upon his students the importance of plumbing the writings of Rabbi Judah Loew of Prague (MaHaRaL), the sixteenth century mystic philosopher. (See *Ozar Igrot Kodesh* [Brooklyn, 1988], letters 252, 275 on pp. 305, 335 concerning Loew's *Netivot Olam*.) Whether this attachment to MaHaRaL sprang from the HaBaD tradition or was Levine's own innovation, I have been unable to ascertain. MaHaRaL's voluminous literary oeuvre never became the subject of formal study in Lubavitch the way it did among the Polish hasidim (followers of Rabbi Simha Bunem of Przysucha). A notable exception to this rule is the attention lavished on MaHaRaL in Zemah Zedek's *Derekh Mizvotekha, mizvat ha'amanat elohut*, chap. 3 and *shoresh mizvat ha-tefillah*, chap. 30. Inter alia, see letter of RaSHaB in foreword to *Kuntress u-Maayan*, p. 22. But even these isolated citations show no more than acquaintance with the introduction to one of MaHaRaL's works, *Gevurot Hashem*. In manuscript, Rabbi Dov Baer Shneuri cites the introduction to yet another of MaHaRaL's works, *Tif'eret Israel*. See *Torat Hayyim*, Vol. *Bereshit* (Brooklyn: Kehot, 1993), p. 682. See further Bezalel Safran, "Maharal and Early Hasidism," in *Hasidism: Continuity or Innovation?* (Cambridge, Mass.: Harvard University Press, 1988), concerning Rabbi Menahem Mendel of Vitebsk, and the glosses of Rabbi Israel, the Maggid of Kozienice published at the conclusion to Loew's *Be'er ha-Golah* (London: L. Honig and Sons,1960). I might add that MaHaRaL (*Netivot 'Olam*, beg. *Netiv ha-Teshuvah*) is cited by yet a third disciple of Dov Baer of Mezhirech, Jacob Joseph of Ostraha. See his *Rav Yevi* (Brody, 1874), *Hiddushim*.

The issue of Shneur Zalman's descent from MaHaRaL of Prague is not germane to our discussion.

67. Heilman, *Beit Rabbi*, II, pp. 193-197 [Hebrew pagination 97a-99a].

68. For details, see Azriel Zelig Slonim, "Hebron ve-HaBaD," in ed. Oded Avissar, *Sefer Hebron* (Jerusalem: Keter, 1970), pp. 117-120.

69. Introduction to Dov Baer Schneuri, *Torat Hayyim, Bereshit*, p. vii.

70. Psalms 36:10.

71. Cf. conclusion to *Idra Zuta* in *Zohar*, III, 296b.

72. See Introduction to D. B. Shneuri, *Shaarei Orah* (Brooklyn: Kehot, 1979), 2a.

73. In Hebrew numerology, *Zemah Zedek* has the same value as *Menahem Mendel*. This work should not be confused with the earlier collection of responsa by Menahem Mendel Krochmal.

74. Letter of J. I. Schneersohn to S. Z. Shmutkin, dated 8 Ellul, 1939, reprinted in *Torah Or* (Brooklyn: Kehot, 1972), p. 143.

75. H. E. Bichovsky, publisher's introduction to *Derekh Mizvotekha* (Poltava, 1911). See also J. I. Schneersohn's letter, ibid., n. 3.

76. It seems well established that Rabbi Hayyim of Volozhin did not hold his master's views concerning the hasidim. See Heilman, *Beit Rabbi*, I, introduction, pp. 10-11; text, pp. 79, 133 [Heb. pagination 40a, 67a]; Anonymous, *RaMaH Otiyot*, p. 43, par. 170; M. M. Yoshor, *He-Hafez Hayyim* (Tel Aviv: Nezah, 1959), II, p. 579; R. Asher Hakohen of Tiktin, *Orhot Hayyim /Keter Rosh* with commentary *Ohalei Hayyim* by Elijah Landau (Jerusalem, n.d.), last page concerning Baal Shem Tov.

77. M. M. Yoshor, *He-Hafez Hayyim* I, p. 581; Hayyim Mordecai Perlov, *Likkutey Sippurim*, pp. 104-105.

Baruch Halevi Epstein recalls the impact made on Vilna's scholars by Rabbi Menahem Mendel's visit there in 1835. See Epstein, *Mekor Baruch* (Vilna: Romm, 1928), Vol. III, pp. 1285-1289 [643-645 in Hebrew pagination]. Specifically, there seems to have existed a relationship between Rabbi Menahem Mendel of Lubavitch and the chief justice of Vilna, Rabbi Abraham Abele Pasvaler. See Perlov, p. 100 and the volume of Pasvaler's responsa, *Be'er Abraham* (Jerusalem: Makhon Yerushalayim, 1980), S. D. Movshovits ed., pp. 345-348.

78. Baruch Halevi Epstein, *Mekor Baruch* , p. 1237 [619 in Hebrew pagination], citing his father, Rabbi Yehiel Mikhel Halevi Epstein of Novohrodok, author of *Arukh ha-Shulhan*.

79. MaHaRaSH (*Zemah Zedek*'s youngest son, Samuel) told a hasid: "Divine love and fear can be attained more in *Torah Or*; knowledge, in *Likkutei Torah*" (*RaMaH Otiyot*, p. 13, par. 61).

80. Shneur Zalman of Liady, *Likkutei Torah* (Brooklyn: Kehot, 1972), endnotes, p. 69a, citing *Torat Shalom*, p. 237.

81. However, in a letter to Rabbi I. J. Yaabez of Jerusalem, appended to Vol. II of *Pele Yo'ez* (Brooklyn: 1990), p. 222, the author, Rabbi Mordecai Dov Twersky of Hornosteipel (a descendent of Rabbi Dov Baer of Lubavitch) refers to the passage concerning Lubavitch in *Mishkenot le-Abir Yaakov* as "false testimony."

82. Yizhak Eizik Halevy Epstein, *Shnei ha-Me'orot* (Poltava: Widow and Sons Rabinowitz, 1918); photo reprint (Brooklyn: Kehot, 1971), pp. 218-219 (in Hebrew pagination 109b-110a).

83. Hillel Halevi of Paritch, *Maamar Hirkavta Enosh le-Roshenu* (Jerusalem: Gal Einai, 1984), ed. Rabbi Yizhak Ginsburgh. Rabbi Hillel bases his state-

ment on a passage in Rabbi Hayyim Vital's *Shaarei Kedusha*. Cf. Rabbi Shelomo Zalman of Kopyst, *Derushim Yekarim* (Vilna: 1903), 3b: "There is found in the writings of ARI (Rabbi Isaac Luria), of blessed memory, that the revelation of the soul in man is higher than the revelation of Elijah (*giluy Eliyahu*) and the Holy Spirit (*ruah ha-kodesh*)."

84. See Bezalel Naor, "The Curtains of the Tabernacle: R. Shelomo Zalman of Kopyst," *Orot / A Multidisciplinary Journal of Judaism*, I (1991), pp. 33-41.

85. The writer Fishel Shneurson, a grandson of the Retchitser Rebbe, relates childood memories of his grandfather's noble behavior during a pogrom, in his story "Be-ma'avak ha-kolot."

86. A volume of his teachings entitled *Shemen la-Maor* was published posthumously in Kefar Habad, Israel in 1964. SHeMeN is an acrostic for "Shemariah Noah."

87. See Hillel Zeitlin, "Di svivah in velkher s'iz oisgevoksen der Rogatchover Iluy zt"l," *Der Moment* (Warsaw) 27: 63, 69 (March 13, 1936). An English translation by Bezalel Naor, "The Milieu in Which the Rogatchover Iluy zt"l Grew Up," appeared in *Chasidic Historical Review* 2:1 (June-July 1997), pp. 26-31. See there p. 30. M. M. Yoshor, *He-Hafez Hayyim* II, p. 592, n. 9, writes that through Rabbi Shelomo Zalman of Kopyst's intervention, Rosen was appointed hasidic rabbi of Dvinsk in 1889.

88. See Bezalel Naor, "The Curtains of the Tabernacle," p. 35. Rav Kook's mentor in HaBaD hasidism was Rabbi Yehezkel Yanover, leader of the hasidim in Grieva, Latvia, Kook's hometown. Outside the Rebbe himself, Rabbi Yehezkel was considered the outstanding interpreter of HaBaD in the Kopyster circle. Some of his interpretations of *Tanya* are recorded in Abraham Zevi Brudna, *Kuntress Likkutim Be'urim* (Jerusalem, 1922). For biographical details concerning Rabbi Yehezkel, see Heilman, *Beit Rabbi*, III, pp. 254-255 (Hebrew, 127b-128a).

89. In his youth, Zeitlin beheld the Retchitser. See Hillel Zeitlin, *Al Gevul Shnei Olamot* (Tel-Aviv: Yavneh, 1965), pp. 198-199.

90. Zevin and Telushkin were in their youth adherents of Bobroisk. Rabbi Telushkin, a native of Bobroisk, relates that he studied in the "kibbutz" of Rabbi Shemariah Noah and was ordained by him. See Nissan Telushkin, *Tohorat Mayim* (Brooklyn: Kehot, 1990), p. 355.

91. A. Litvin (pseudonym of S. Hurwitz) has described the wretched state

of Liady after the demise of Isaac Dov Baer. It seems his son Shakhna was unable to attract a following. See Litvin's travelogue, "In Shtetl fun'm 'Alten Rebbe'n'" in his collection, *Yiddishe Neshomos* [Yiddish] (New York: Arbeter Ring, 1917), Vol. VI.

92. A facsimile edition was brought out by the hasidic researcher J. Mondshein in Kefar Habad, Israel in 1991. See also Bezalel Naor, "Two Types of Prayer," *Tradition,* 25 (3), Spring 1991, pp. 26-34.

Rabbi Shalom Rivkin of St. Louis, MO is in possession of Ladier discourses his father Rabbi Moshe Dov Baer Rivkin recorded in his youth as a hasid of Liady. (When the Ladier died, Rivkin transferred his allegiance to Rabbi Shalom Dov Baer (RaSHaB) of Lubavitch. It was Rivkin who wrote the account of RaSHaB's last days, *Ashkavta de-Rabbi.*) Klau Library of Hebrew Union College, Cincinnati, possesses discourses of Hayyim Shneur Zalman of Liady, designated as ms. 738.

93. Dov Katz, *Tenu'at ha-Mussar,* Vol. I, (Jerusalem, 1982), pp. 335-336. See also p. 334 for another interesting encounter between the representatives of the two different spiritual traditions. Rabbi Israel Salanter's view may be summed up by the following saying of his: "Both *mitnagdim* and *hasidim* are in error. The *mitnagdim* err in thinking they have no *rebbe*; the *hasidim* are mistaken in thinking they have a *rebbe*" (Ibid., p. 310). M. M. Yoshor, I, p. 320, n. 1, attributes to MaHaRaSH the following appraisal of Salanter: "God took pity on the poor *mitnagdim* and lowered to them one soul of a hasidic rebbe, but the *mitnagdim* were unworthy of it and derived no benefit therefrom."

94. See A. I. Kook, *Igrot ha-RAYaH* (Jerusalem: Mossad Harav Kook, 1962), pp. 34-36.

95. Hayyim Eliezer Bichovski reports the high esteem in which Rabbi Meir Simcha held the rebbe of Bobroisk at the time of their meeting in 1910. See *Kitvei ha-RHE Bichovski*, p. 154.

96. They believed that in this way the detested post of *kazyonniy ravvin*, "crown rabbi," could be abolished.

97. Yoshor, *He-Hafez Hayyim*, I, pp. 347-349.

98. S. B. Schneersohn, *Kuntress u-Maayan*, p. 132.

99. See J. I. Schneersohn, *Sefer ha-Sihot 5701* (Brooklyn: Kehot, 1964), pp. 172-173; Interview with Rabbi S. B. Kowalsky, *Kfar Chabad*, no. 592

(11.04.93), p. 21; Rabbi Meir Berlin, *Fun Volozhin biz Yerushalayim* II New York, 1933), pp. 390-391.

100. Soloveichik was a direct descendant of Rabbi Hayyim of Volozhin, the greatest disciple of the Gaon of Vilna.

101. S. B. Schneersohn, *Ha-Ketav ve-ha-Mikhtav* (New York, 1917). See also the exchange between Rabbi Shelomo Aronson (later Ashkenazic chief rabbi of Tel Aviv) and RaSHaB in Nezhin in 1903. Published in foreword to *Kuntress U-Maayan*, pp. 45-53.

102. Moshe Dov Baer Rivkin, *Ashkavta de-Rabbi* (Brooklyn, 1976), pp. 3-10.

103. Ibid., p. 96.

104. Shalom Dov Baer Scheersohn, *Sefer ha-Ma'amarim 5666* (Brooklyn: Kehot, 1991), p. 432.

105. *Zohar* I, 11b, cited in *Tanya* II, chapter 6 (p. 81b).

106. Menahem Mendel Schneersohn (*Zemah Zedek*), *Derekh Mizvotekha* (Brooklyn: Kehot, 1973), 54b, 124b. It seems the thought originated with Shneur Zalman of Liady. See *Likkutei Torah, Tézé*, 38d, *Lekha Havayah ha-Zedakah* in *Ma'amrei Admor ha-Zaken/Et-halekh Liozno*, published as the introduction to *Selihot 'al-pi Minhag HaBaD* (Brooklyn: Merkoz le-'Inyenei Hinukh, 1986), p. vi. The failure of contemporary academic literature to take note of these sources has led some to mistakenly conclude that for HaBaD, ultimately, this-worldly existence is an illusion.

107. A. Litvin (pseudonym of S. Hurwitz), "Der Letzter Litvisher Guter Yid," in *Yiddishe Neshomos*, Vol. VI.

108. J. I. Schneersohn, *Sefer ha-Sihot 5701*, p. 15.

109. To a Bukharan kabbalist who visited Lubavitch during Menahem Mendel's lifetime, it was apparent the sons lacked their father's knowledge. See A. Litvin, *Yiddishe Neshomos*, Vol. I (New York: Arbeter Ring, 1916), "Der Bukharer Baal Mekubbal." When one of his sons, Joseph Isaac of Avritch, set up court in Poland, the Zemah Zedek wrote him a letter not to become a *rebbe* as he was unworthy of the office (*RaMaH Otiyot*, p. 56, par. 228; Heilman, *Beit Rabbi*, III, p. 245 (Heb. pagination 123a)). On the other hand, Yehiel Mikhel Halevi Epstein praised the Torah scholarship of another of Rabbi Menahem Mendel's sons, Israel Noah of Nezhin. He felt if it were not for the

hasidic tradition thrust upon him, the man would have been better suited to sitting and studying as one of Vilna's *perushim*. See Baruch Halevi Epstein, *Mekor Baruch*, III, p. 1633 [817 in Hebrew pagination]; also Heilman, *Beit Rabbi*, III, pp. 244-245, 250 [Heb. pagination 122b-123a, 125b]. The *Zemah Zedek* said of Rabbi Israel Noah: "*Er iz mein gaon*" (He is my genius). In H. M. Perlov, *Likkutey Sippurim*, p. 135.

In a similar vein, Rabbi Hayyim Abraham Dov Baer Hakohen Levine (known by his followers as "the Angel") wrote: "The truth is that the wisdom of HaBaD is completely hidden; since the holy ark, our master, the *Zemah Zedek* was buried, the wisdom was buried with him" (*Ozar Igrot Kodesh* [Brooklyn: Netivot Olam, 1989], p. 94). This was essentially the position of Shelomo Zalman of Kopyst. His epistle to the *hasidim* after the death of his father in 1867 (referred to as *Ma'amar ha-Ganana*) practically sounds a death-knell on the 150th anniversary of the movement. (Strangely, he gives the approximate date of Baal Shem Tov's revelation as 1718, which would have been BESHT's twentieth, not thirty-sixth birthday, as generally held!) The letter, eventually published posthumously as the introduction to Shelomo Zalman's collected teachings, *Magen Avot*, was hitherto circulated by the *hasidim* in manuscript. See Rabbi Pinhas Hakohen Lintop, "Or ha-Ganuz be-Hokhmat ha-Emet," ed. Y. Suvalski, *Knesset ha-Gedolah* (Warsaw, 1890), I, p. 56. Lintop, though not formally a *hasid* himself, served as the rabbi of the *hasidim* in Birzh, Lithuania. See N. Z. Fridman, *Ozar ha-Rabbanim* (Bnai Berak, 1975), entry 6932.

110. This engineering background stood Rabbi Schneerson in good stead when in 1957 he ruled that with modern technology there was no justification for the Israeli passenger line to violate the Sabbath. See the responsum to him by Rabbi Moses Feinstein, *Igrot Moshe, Orah Hayyim* (New York, 1959), no. 92.

111. *Mishnah, Avot* 4:12. See Rashi *ad locum*.

112. *Sha'arei Orah*, 53a, 51b.

113. The belief in the Rebbe's messianic role was augmented by the fact that he was the seventh generation from Rabbi Shneur Zalman of Liady. The rabbis, in reference to Moses, had said: "All sevenths are beloved." (Moses was the seventh generation from Abraham—Abraham, Isaac, Jacob, Levi, Kehath,

Amram, Moses.) The Polish hasidim had once applied this maxim to Menahem Mendel of Kotzk, the seventh generation from Baal Shem Tov. (Baal Shem Tov, Dov Baer of Mezhirech, Elimelekh of Lizhansk, Jacob Isaac Horowitz, the "Seer" of Lublin, Jacob Isaac of Przysucha, the "Holy Jew," Simha Bunem of Przysucha, Menahem Mendel of Kotzk.)

Dedication

To Reuven Hakohen Alperowitz
Who transmitted the key if not the code

Preface

Rabbi Israel Baal Shem Tov said: "No experience is as powerful as as Hasidism in the beginning."

My earliest initiation into Hasidism took place in the Maine woods. Under the spell of a children's biography of the Baal Shem Tov, that sanctuary of nature celebrated by Henry David Thoreau was permeated with the sprites of the Carpathian Mountains.

My first exposure of any kind to Lubavitch (or Habad) Hasidism was the coming into possession of an ancestor's copy of *Siddur Torah Ohr/Nussach ho-Ari*, published in Vilna before World War II. What struck me about this book was how different its version of prayer was from that in use in school and synagogue. Something about the exotic prayer book suggested itself to the youngster with a feel for language. Only years later would I learn that this particular edition, complete with *Shaar ha-Kollel*, is treasured by Lubavitcher hasidim.

As a child, I felt magnetically drawn to the vanished world of East European Jewry. It became all the more precious in my eyes, and in the eyes of my generation, because it had been brutally liquidated in the inferno of the Holocaust.

Today, once again I feel, as in my childhood, that a precious mystic tradition is threatened by extinction. After two hundred years and seven generations, HaBaD, this most profound and eloquent expression of the genius of Hasidism, is in the throes of a painful moratorium. Yet moratorium is an opportunity for reexamination and retrospection. It is in this spirit that these stories, spanning four decades, are offered.

R.A.

The Pretender

"REUVEN, I RESPECT YOUR JUDGMENT AS A teacher and have to ask you something of utmost importance."

It is my good friend Menahem on the phone. Menahem, professor at a prominent institution, is considered an expert in Habad history. Never have I heard such gravity in his voice.

"What would you think of the following?" It turns out that a young man has visited the university several times over the past months and developed an intimate relationship with Menahem. He claims to have been in psychic communication with the previous *rebbeim* of Habad since puberty. Using him as a medium, they have dictated numerous *maamorim.*[*]

"Do you believe something like this possible?"

"In theory, yes. I do believe in psychic ability, that souls of persons deceased can communicate with the living. As for the Habad tradition in particular, you know as well as I that the Rebbe Rashab made such claims. The Rashab taught *maamorim* of previous generations of *rebbeim* that he heard expounded in heaven."

"The young man claims that the first time it happened he brought the text of the *maamar* to the Rebbe. The Rebbe commanded him to pass on to him all future *maamorim*. Over the years, he has regularly brought the Rebbe these mediumistic *maamorim*, to which the Rebbe adds his own footnotes."

"Has he ever shown you any of these texts?"

"No."

"Now listen to this. My young friend claims that since that first incursion years ago, the Rebbe has received from his teachers detailed reports of his spiritual progress. The Rebbe monitors closely all his movements."

"Fascinating."

"The reason I called you, Reuven, is because today he revealed to me the full extent of it. He says that the

---

[*] *maamorim,* mystical discourses, singular *maamar*.

Rebbe ordained him to be his successor. In one of their private sessions, the Rebbe lay his hands upon his head and said to him: "My head will be your head, my heart will be your heart . . ." I'm convinced he's telling the truth. Am I a dupe or is this really possible?"

"Let me ask you a few questions. First, is your young friend a descendant of the Alter Rebbe?"

"No."

"Would you consider him major league in Talmud?"

"No."

"My hunch is the man is a fraud. How could the Rebbe name as his successor someone who is not a member of the "royal family"? And given the premium the Rebbe places on Talmudic learning, how could he entrust the movement to an individual whose scholarship is at most mediocre? It seems, Menahem, that he has swept you off your feet with his charisma and that you have suspended objective judgment."

I thought I had cured my friend of a fantasy. I was mistaken.

A few weeks later I bumped into Menahem in the library. He quickly took me aside. "You were wrong. This is on the level. The real thing. He has revealed to me intimate details that only the Rebbe's successor could know."

"Why didn't the Rebbe declare him publicly as his successor?"

"The Rebbe told him remorsefully that he cannot do that for his own good."

In weeks to come, the Rebbe's health deteriorated drastically. Menahem's friend confided that he was in psychic communication with the Rebbe even as he lie in a vegetative state in Beth Israel Hospital. "There is very little *gashmiyus* (physical nature) left to the Rebbe. He is practically pure *ruchniyus* (spiritual nature) at this point."

One Sunday morning as I was showering, my daughter pounded on the bathroom door. "The Lubavitcher Rebbe died." I could not believe my ears.

It was true. The radio in the next room blared the news. After a long, hopeless illness of several months, the Rebbe had finally expired.

In the aftermath of the Rebbe's death, the entire Jewish world and I waited for news of a successor. The Rebbe had died childless. The blow came a few days later when Rabbi Yehuda Krinsky, the Rebbe's personal secretary, called a press conference at which he read the last will and testament. There would be no successor to the Lubavitcher Rebbe. After two hundred years and seven generations, the Schneersohn dynasty was finished.

That night I got Menahem on the line. "What happened? You said your friend was the pretender to the throne."

"Krinsky's posturing. He read *a* will. But there's another will."

"What?"

"That's right. At different times the Rebbe dictated various wills. Tomorrow you will read in the press details of a totally different will."

Sure enough. The next day the Jewish press provided the full text of an entirely different will. But nowhere did it mention word of a successor.

The next night I was back on the phone with Menahem. "I read the other will. It too does not mention your friend."

"I know. My friend assures me there is yet a third will that addresses the issue of succession. The problem is, those who know of its existence are too intimidated to come forward."

As days passed, hope of a successor vanished.

The last time I saw Menahem, I asked him what he thought, now that it was all over.

"I still think he might have been telling the truth. There are things he revealed to me for which there is no other explanation."

Hashgocho Protis

THE 18TH OF *ELLUL*. THE BIRTHDAY OF TWO GREAT luminaries, the Baal Shem Tov, founder of Hasidism, and the *Baal ha-Tanya*, Rav Shneur Zalman of Liady, founder of the school of Hasidism known as Habad. In previous years, this had been a joyous occasion. This year a great vacuum is felt, for a few months prior the Rebbe of Habad, Menahem Mendel Schneerson, passed to his eternal reward.

I am standing on the steps of 770 Eastern Parkway, which had served as the Rebbe's synagogue. A wedding is in process. In attendance are the notables of the Lubavitch community, prominent rabbis. They have just called to the *huppah* to read the Rebbe's letter, Rabbi Yitshak Springer, *mashpi'a* of the Lubavitch Yeshiva. He reads a few words, then falls silent. This sequence repeats itself a few times. I think

I know the reason why. He is struck by the irony of the situation. The Rebbe is no longer alive. Springer is reading the letter of a ghost.

As Rabbi Springer emerges from under the canopy I catch my first glimpse of him. I haven't seen the man for a quarter of a century. His beard has turned white. Sure enough, tears roll down his cheeks.

My own vision fills with memories of a yeshiva student desperately searching for God. Every Friday he would study *Tanya* in the privacy of the home of the local Lubavitch *shaliah* (emissary) in Baltimore, a young enthusiastic teacher by the name of Yitshak Springer. Springer married the daughter of the teacher of the Rebbe, Reb Zalman Vilenkin. He taught Schneerson when the latter was a youngster in Russia. Upon Vilenkin's arrival in America, he paid a visit to his former student, now the world-famous Rebbe. The Rebbe asked Vilenkin to be seated. He refused out of respect for the Rebbe. So the Rebbe too stood. Now it was a stalemate. Thereupon Vilenkin acquiesced to sit.

At a certain point, evidently Rabbi Springer felt that I had advanced so in my study of Hasidism that I should transfer over to the Lubavitch Yeshiva. He put me on a bus to New York and told me to instruct Rabbi Hayyim Mordecai Chodakov, the Rebbe's secretary, that I should be granted a *yehidut* (private audience) with the Rebbe that very night.

Late that evening I arrive in the office of the secretariat. Upon hearing my unusual request, Rabbi Chodakov (who had been a member of the Latvian government before World War II) is chagrined: "People have made appointments months in advance. How can you just barge in like that?!"

I stick to my guns. "Rabbi Yitshak Springer said I must see the Rebbe tonight."

Finally, a compromise is struck. Chodakov will hand the Rebbe a letter from me and give me his reply the next morning, Friday. Hurriedly I spill my guts onto a sheet of paper handed me. In literary Hebrew I pen the following lines:

> *His Holiness the Rebbe, may he live –*
>
> *I have been searching for God for many years and still, to my pain, feel that I am very far from Godliness. What must I do, which path must I pursue to reach my goal in life?*
>
> *Reuven son of Shprintsa*

"Fine. Now where will you sleep?"

"There's a park bench outside."

"Do you know anyone in Crown Heights?"

"My eighth grade teacher."

Rabbi Chodakov rings up my former teacher.

A few minutes later I am on his doorstep. He greets me in bathrobe.

"What's this all about?"

"I am here to enroll in the Lubavitch Yeshiva."

"That's a terrible idea. I sent you to the yeshiva in Baltimore. For you to enroll in Lubavitch would be a mistake. Mark my words, tomorrow the Rebbe himself will advise you it's a mistake. I am not the Rebbe but I am close enough to his way of thinking to predict that. You'll see."

The thought passes through my mind that this man should be booted out of the Lubavitch movement for heresy.

The next morning, bright and early, I am in Rabbi Chodakov's office. He guides me into an inner cubicle. Sitting with me at a table, he unveils the Rebbe's reply in pencil to my question.

> *He should study in the yeshiva where he is presently studying, diligently and assiduously.*

The Rebbe also recommended that my *tefillin** be checked. (I took them to a scribe on the Lower East Side. It turned out they were ritually unfit.)

Having read the reply, I was ready to storm out of the office. The answer struck me as wrong on two

---

**Tefillin* are the small leather boxes containing scriptural passages worn on the left arm and forehead during morning weekday prayers.

accounts. First, I didn't think going back to the same yeshiva was the solution to my problem. Second, how could the man respond so cooly, so prosaically to such a warm, impassioned plea for help?

Over the next hour, Rabbi Chodakov tried to explicate to me the Rebbe's answer. (To this day I don't know whether this was the Rebbe's idea or his own.) He told me the story of Rabbi Akiva. Akiva had been an ignorant shepherd until age forty. He observed how the drops of water flowing over a rock gradually bore a hole in it. He reasoned that by the same principle, the waters of Torah could gradually enter even his stony consciousness. Enlightenment would not come overnight. It would be a gradual process. In addition, Rabbi Chodakov strongly suggested that I share my Torah knowledge with others, that over the summer I teach classes.

Words of wisdom are wasted on youth. I was growing impatient. I told him I must be off to Boston.

"Why not stay here Shabbos? There will be a *farbrengen* (hasidic gathering) tomorrow when it will be possible to hear the Rebbe speak."

In so many words, I let Chodakov understand that if it was the Rebbe's intention that I stay put, he should have said so. As it stood, his message clearly, unequivocally pointed in the opposite direction. I was off to Boston for the Sabbath.

Picture a young man with a straw hat, dark glasses and a cigar jutting out of his mouth. His mood is diffident and ornery. This was me on a Trailways bus to Boston. As I was seated in the rear of the bus, passengers kept turning around to scour at the source of the foul fumes. Suddenly, someone slipped me a business card:

I have no money.
I have no *mazal.*
All I have is *hashgocho protis.*

I look to my left side. There sits a clean-shaven grandfatherly type. A simple-looking old Jew.

For the next twenty minutes he tells me his life story:

"I am from Detroit. My father was a Gerer hasid. At a young age I rebelled. I left home and religion. Later, I heard my father died. I came back home. I took Papa's *tallis* (prayer shawl) and *tefillin* and put them on. Mama cried for joy."

"Some years later I married and settled in Crown Heights, Brooklyn. I joined the Conservative synagogue. One day something possessed me to enter the small hasidic synagogue that had formed in our neighborhood. There was some sort of celebration going on. I stood at the very back. The man leading the celebration motioned me forward to the dais. He asked me my name. In that and subsequent private conversations, he explained to me the concept of *hashgocho protis*, divine supervision, how the universe works."

"Eventually I reached such a level of commitment to Judaism that I told the Rebbe of my plans to leave the Conservative synagogue. The Rebbe vetoed the idea. He said I must remain a member there to influence the other members of the congregation, which I did. My children, thank God, have grown up Orthodox and I am on my way to visit them for Shabbos."

"So son, the motto you see emblazoned on my card is the philosophy I learned from the Lubavitcher Rebbe. He taught me *hashgocho protis*."

At a certain stop far outside Boston, my co-passenger descended from the bus. I never said a word the entire time he spoke. I am still too speechless to evaluate his message.

Rabbi Menahem Mendel Schneerson
[1902-1994]

"And I am the Last"

THE LONG-AWAITED *YEHIDUT*, THE PRIVATE AUDIence, with the world-renowned Lubavitcher Rebbe is finally taking place. At last alone with the Rebbe! The Rebbe reveals his true warmth and love. No more formalism.

He begins to explain the kabbalistic notion that in each generation there lives a soul with the potential to be the Messiah. Any one of these given individuals could be the Messiah if only the right conditions prevail. The candidate himself would have to remain unsullied; the generation would have to merit Messiah's coming.

The Rebbe begins to paint a picture of those many Messiahs-in-potentia, each tragically flawed in some way, each destined for greatness but doomed to failure. As the Rebbe speaks, I behold the faces of these Promethean figures: the mighty general Bar Kochba defeated by the Romans, the mystic Shabbetai Zevi who ends as a Muslim apostate, the renegade rebbe Dov Baer Friedman of Liova converted to Haskalah. I see the march of generations. I peer into those holy, heroic, tortured visages until I am driven to tears and rage and madness.

When I can bear it no longer, I find myself once again opposite the Rebbe. Having finished his discourse, he smiles, his eyes expressing infinity, and says: "And I am the last."

The next day I can hardly function on the mundane plane. I am awed by the power of the dream and bewildered by its implications. It is the proverbial mishmash of wheat and chaff. Dov Baer of Liova a Messiah-in-potentia. Humph! All I have read tells me he was a small-time rebbe, a mediocre mind.

To unburden myself, I relate my dream to a Yemenite student of mysticism in Hebron. I begin to repaint the visages of the numerous failed, fallen Messiahs. He pales with fright and can hear no more.

Ten years later I am lying in bed in Greenville, Maine where I have beat a summer retreat from the heat and tension of New York. It is late at night. I am alone reading the historian Samuel Werses' book on Haskalah and Sabbatianism. I come across an 1869 letter of the venerable Rabbi Hayyim Halberstam of

Sanz to the Rebbe of Vizhnitz, in which he explains why he persecutes the thousands of followers of the Ruzhin dynasty. "Some maintain that the renegade (Dov Baer Friedman) is the Messiah, bad on the outside and good on the inside; others purport that there was an assumption and his double did the deeds—and other idiocies such as once claimed the followers of Shabbetai Zevi." For that reason, the revered talmudist had seen necessary to raise a hue and cry.

I get out of bed and look through the window. The night is black. How was it possible for me to dream that a decade ago?

I emerge from my reverie to the present. It is but a month since the Lubavitcher Rebbe passed away in Beth Israel Hospital in Manhattan. At death, he weighed not quite sixty pounds and had lost most of his beard. He had been brain-dead for months. To this day his followers sing, "Long live our master, our teacher and rabbi, King Messiah for ever and ever."

Truly the last.

The Last Lubavitcher

HE STOOD BESIDE ME AT THE WEDDING CANOPY, the *huppah*. A short, wizened man. At a certain point in the wedding ceremony, where he felt the young American Lubavitchers had overdone it, he hissed to me: "*Narish!*" "Foolish!" His years, his entire being bespoke a foreignness.

"Are you from Russia?"

"Yes."

"From which town?"

He looked at me suspiciously. "Were you also once from Russia? Do you know Russia?"

"We came from White Russia."

Pacified, he responded, "Lubavitch." And with a mischievous grin he added, "Did you hear of Lubavitch?"

As the ceremony continued for an inordinately

long time, we had opportunity to *schmuess*. It turned out my interlocutor was born in Lubavitch and grew up in Leningrad—of late St. Petersburg. Later, I discovered his father had been a *gabbai*, an attendant, of the Rebbe Rashab in Lubavitch. Remarks my acquaintance had made in the past, calling for a return to the *Tanya*'s ideal of the *oved hashem*, one who serves God, had been misinterpreted in certain quarters and had required clarification.

The master of ceremonies was now calling upon the assemblage to reaffirm their faith, at which cue they immediately burst into the triplicate chanting of *Yehi Adoneinu*:

"Long live our master, our teacher, our rabbi, King Messiah for ever and ever!"

As I walked off, I wondered how the old man was faring this latest innovation.

Spinoza and the *Alter Rebbe*

I HAD JUST COMPLETED MY COLLEGE STUDIES AND arrived in New York City to start a new life. At age twenty-two, the possibilities seemed infinite.

My first night in town remains with me as a beautiful memory. There was a gathering of friends in my honor in a West Side apartment. Later that evening, we were a threesome walking through the brilliantly lit plaza of Lincoln Center. With Isaac on my left and Michael on my right, I was surrounded by the security of lifelong friendship. Despite the cold of the New York winter, I felt a warm glow inside.

The next morning I was informed by Isaac that I would have to find another place to stay. He was heading home for the month-long intersession and intended to close down the apartment. After a momentary sense of loss, I hailed a cab to take me to the Washington Heights address of a great aunt and uncle.

Eventually I would be expelled from there too, but by then I had gotten my bearings sufficiently to rent a basement flat in Brooklyn and enroll in a graduate program of studies in Jewish Philosophy. But what had become of Michael?

Since that first, initial rendezvous, Michael had disappeared off the face of the earth. Repeated phone calls to his parents' home proved of no avail. As days turned into weeks, and weeks into months, with yet no sign of Michael, my heart filled with perplexity and foreboding. Michael had left me that night with an intriguing tale. Perhaps that alone should have alerted me that something was amiss.

He claimed to have seen in a vision two faces: Baruch or Benedict Spinoza, the philosopher of Amsterdam, and Shneur Zalman, the *Alter Rebbe*, founder of Habad Hasidism. In the vision, the two faces, of the heretic and of the saint, coalesced, until Michael was seeing in the eyes of the *Baal ha-Tanya*,* the eyes of Spinoza!

---

* "The author of *Tanya*," Rabbi Shneur Zalman of Liady.

Life in New York was settling into a challenging rhythm. By day, Talmudic studies in Brooklyn; by night, graduate courses in Manhattan. Through happenstance meetings, a new circle of friends de-veloped. At the time, New York seemed the most exciting place on earth.

In graduate school, I took a course in the writings of Rav Kook. Kook, who had served as Ashkenazic chief rabbi of mandatory Palestine, created a mystical system of philosophy that is unparalleled in modern Jewish thought. His unitive, evolving vision of the cosmos expresses itself in poetic consciousness, so that one professor has likened his work to a cross between Sri Aurobindo and Walt Whitman.

As I delved more deeply into Rav Kook's voluminous writings, I found myself beginning to see things in that mystical mode. Reading Rav Kook and looking around Fort Tryon Park or Brooklyn Botanical Gardens, I could glimpse the harmony in creation of which he sang.

Kook's mother's people had been Lubavitcher hasidim. In his hometown of Grieva, Latvia he imbibed the mystical teachings from Reb Chatskel Yanover, the famed *mashpi'a* (teacher of Habad hasidism). Even after he went on to pursue rabbinic studies at the Volozhin Yeshiva, it seems the initial outlook of the *Tanya* never left him. Rav Kook describes a world drenched in divinity, where God may be discovered in every leaf and rock.

One day in my rented room below street level, I came across the following passage in Rav Kook's *Lights of Holiness*:

> Less enervating than the monotheistic view is the Spinozist pantheistic explanation (of reality), as refined in the Habad school of Hasidism, that there is nothing outside of God.

Was this not Michael's vision?

June. Summer had finally come to New York. Light was streaming through my basement window. Good days were ahead. I could feel it in my bones. A knock on the door heralded a visitor. Standing on the other side was cosmic explorer Michael, bag in hand. Could he stay with me for a few days? He had just been released from a mental ward, where, to use his expression, he had been "incarcerated" for the past months.

Over the Sabbath meal, I finally broached the subject.

"Michael, do you remember what you told me that last night?"

"No. What?"

"You related to me a vision of Spinoza being transmogrified into the *Baal ha-Tanya*."

"Did I say that?"

"You saw Spinoza's eyes in the portrait of the *Baal ha-Tanya*."

He laughed. "Their eyes are totally different. I must really have been crazy."

Rabbi Zevi Yehuda Hakohen Kook
[1891-1982]

The Misnaged

Zevi Yehuda Kook was the only son of Abraham Isaac Kook, first Ashkenazic chief rabbi of Palestine.

His had been a lonely life. He delayed marriage until he was already in his thirties. Then he was a widower in middle age. And childless. The union with Hava Leah Hutner of Warsaw was without issue. And despite, or perhaps because of his solitude, he was able to bestow love upon hundreds, maybe thousands, of disciples.

He devoted a lifetime to editing and publishing his father's literary legacy. He was constantly held up for comparison to his father—and found wanting. He lacked his father's brilliance, his charisma. When in the aftermath of the Six Day War, he founded the *Gush*

Emunim (Bloc of the Faithful) to settle Judea and Samaria, this was added to by now a long list of "sins."

My own relationship with Rav Zevi Yehuda Kook commenced in the eighty-seventh year of his life. I was a newlywed in my twenties. Recently arrived in Jerusalem, I heard from a French *ger zedek* (righteous convert to Judaism), Professor Abraham Livni (Blanc), about Rav Kook's son. Having been himself a spiritual seeker, in his youth joining a band of Braslav hasidim and in early manhood traveling to Europe for secular studies, Rav Zevi Yehuda was able to relate to others' search. Of late, his specialty was French *baalei teshuvah* (returnees to the Jewish tradition).

The next evening I was in Rav Zevi Yehuda's apartment at 30 Ovadiah Street in the Geulah section of town. He had inherited from his father the tradition of transforming one's private abode into the home of the Jewish People. The surroundings were simple, bare and austere. Yeshiva students seemed to fill every cranny of the modest apartment. I was informed by Yossi Badihi, the Yemenite student who took care of the Rav, that a *rosh yeshiva* from Switzerland was in with him. My bride and I waited patiently. Eventually the door opened and a Rabbi Botchko of Montreux emerged—backwards. Then, framed in the doorway, we beheld a short cherub with luminous visage. This was the much calumniated Zevi Yehuda Kook.

Our very first meeting cemented our relationship. It was uncanny. I felt so sure in that relationship that in days to come I would share with Rav Zevi Yehudah entries from my diary—material which eventually became the backbone of a book.

"I see that you have been ensnared (*nitfasta*) by Hasidism," was his verdict upon reading a certain passage in my notebook. The word "ensnared" was strange to my ears. I was certain he must be joking. He was not. He proceeded to recount the shortcomings of Hasidism, the cultic aspects, the derogation of Torah learning.

I thought surely this was a passing mood. Had not his father dedicated himself to the task of fusing the two traditions, of the Vilna Gaon's disciples on the one hand, and of the Baal Shem Tov's disciples on the other? I was mistaken.

There was no budging Rav Zevi Yehuda from the subject. Having discovered my "ensnarement," every time we met now he diverted the conversation to his *bete noir*—Hasidism. As a result, our relationship suffered. Disciples related similar experiences.

Years later, I came across a published essay of Rav Zevi Yehuda entitled, "The Prince of the Torah of *Hesed* (Love)," in praise of Rabbi Joseph Isaac Schneersohn (while the latter yet lived!). In a broadsweep of cosmic history, commencing with the two millennia of Chaos (*Tohu*), continuing with the two millennia of Torah and culminating in the two millennia of Messiah, Zevi Yehuda Kook views the role of Habad as paving the way from the aeon of Torah to the age of Messiah.

> There was sent the gigantic soul of the godly genius, our master Rabbi Shneur Zalman . . . By the appearance of the Prince of Torah of *Hesed* (Love), divine supervision paved the transition of worlds and epochs from the millennia of Torah to the millennia of the Days of Messiah.

What, then, was Rav Zevi Yehuda seeing? Had the psychic who so accurately predicted the victories of the Six Day War, foreseen something frightening and ominous? Time and time again, Rav Kook drummed into me this, his final message: "The *Gaon* (of Vilna) knew what he was doing . . ."

Yaakov Alperowitz,
father of Reuven [Robert], my great uncle.
[1853?-1930?]

The Confession

CAN YOU REMEMBER THE THRILL OF DRIVING YOUR first car? I was a college student cruising on a lovely summer day. I happened to go down French Street. Sitting on their porch, I spied my great aunt and uncle. How forlorn they looked, how forgotten by the world. I could not pass them by.

They seemed genuinely pleased to have me join them on the porch. They had aged so since last I saw them. Usually it would be my Aunt Faya, talkative and coquettish, who would maintain the conversation, while Uncle Ruvke would bury himself in the Yiddish newspaper. Ruvke (endearing for Reuven) was a tight-lipped retired retail merchant. A free-thinker with mildly socialist leanings, he was the farthest thing from an Orthodox Jew. In Maine, Ruvke had become Robert, a Yankee sportsman. Today, as he sat on his porch looking out into the distance, he revealed a past incongruous, incredible.

"I was the favorite son of my father. He sent me to study in my uncle's yeshiva." To my amazement Uncle Ruvke now began to rattle off rabbinic sayings: *Odom koreiv etsel atsmay*. "A man is close to himself." *Im ta'azveini yaim, yaimayim a'azveko*. "If you leave me for one day, I will leave you for two."

"A few months more and I would have received my *semicha* (rabbinic ordination). Instead I ran away to America. My poor father was devastated, heart-broken."

I could see that Ruvke's rocker had taken off from the French Street launch pad and was converging on Dolhinov, White Russia.

"My father and I made the pilgrimage to Lubavitch for *Shavu'os* (Festival of Pentecost). Our family were Lubavitcher hasidim, you know." (Ruvke, how could I have known that? I thought our family were Maine woodsmen.) "The hasidim were dancing hand on shoulder . . ."

Ruvke started to say something about my great-grandfather Zalman Mendel, then abruptly stopped himself, once again freezing into silence. Zalman Mendel Hakohen Alperovich had been born April 14,

1869 in Sosenka, a village a stone's throw from the town of Ilya. What was Ruvke about to reveal? I shall never know.

What could I say? I was dumbfounded. When I stole away from *yeshiva* to study *Tanya* by the stream in the woods, did I know my ancestors had been followers of Lubavitch? When I searched that little book for answers to the ultimate questions of existence, could I have divined therein my gnarled roots? Somehow I made my way back from the porch to the car.

On my next visit home, I learned that Uncle Ruvke had died.

Circles

THIS WOULD BE MY FIRST TIME ATTENDING THE lecture of the *rosh yeshiva* (dean of the yeshiva). I grabbed a seat up front so I could hear clearly every word. I was curious what he looked like. I had heard so much about him.

His delivery was stoic, expressionless. What struck me was his peculiar pronunciation of Yiddish. It sounded vaguely familiar to my ear. All other impressions of that first *shiur* (talmudic lecture) have since faded.

The *rosh yeshiva* was Rabbi Jacob Isaac Ruderman. His father, Judah Leib Futterfass (Ruderman, as many Jewish names in Russia, was an invention) had been a Lubavitcher hasid. Together, father and son had made the pilgrimage to Lubavitch to behold the Rebbe Rashab in all his kingly splendor.

At a young age, Jacob Isaac enrolled in the famed Slabodka Yeshiva. A child prodigy, he soon came to the attention of the *rosh yeshiva*, the saintly Nathan Zevi Finkel. Orphaned by the untimely death of Judah Leib, Jacob Isaac looked to Rabbi Finkel as a father figure. Raised in the *rosh yeshiva*'s home, he thoroughly imbibed the Mussar spirit of Slabodka with its unique emphasis on *gadlut ha-adam*, man's greatness.

When it came time to wed, Rabbi Ruderman married a granddaughter of one of Rabbi Israel Salanter's disciples, the Maecenas Shraga Frank. His uncles by marriage were the greatest Lithuanian *roshei yeshivos*, Rabbi Isser Zalman Meltzer of Slutsk (later of Jerusalem) and Rabbi Moses Mordecai Epstein of Slabodka (later of Hebron). Meltzer's son-in-law, Rabbi Aaron Kotler of Kletsk (later of Lakewood) thus became a cousin to Rabbi Ruderman by marriage.

Rabbi Jacob Isaac Halevi Ruderman, *rosh yeshiva* of Ner Israel in Baltimore, was thoroughly weaned of all Habad influence. Or was he?

Throughout his life, he retained a fondness for the small book *Tanya*, having the custom of taking it with him on trips. When my own first book appeared in print, heavily influenced as it was by *Tanya* and other more expansive works of the *Alter Rebbe*, the *rosh yeshiva* said to me: "Based on what I see in your *sefer* (sacred book), you could be a rebbe."

Years passed. Home was now Israel. I was sitting in the Jerusalem salon of Rabbi Nathan Kaminetsky to comfort him in his time of mourning for his illustrious father, Rabbi Jacob Kaminetsky, *rosh yeshiva* of Torah Vodaath. Seated beside me were admirers of "Reb Yaakov" of all ages. There happened in an old timer who presently resided in rural Zichron Yaakov, in the north of the country. It turned out he had been a student of Rabbi Ruderman in Baltimore half a century ago. As a young man, fears of making a go of it in the world pressed in on him. When he informed the Rosh Yeshiva of his decision to leave yeshiva for a Jewish-owned university, he was referred to Rav Yaakov Kaminetsky for advice. Evidently, the counsel he received lasted him in good stead, for he had just travelled several hours to convey his belated gratitude to the son of "Reb Yaakov" whom he had never in his life met.

The conversation began to lag. Somehow it came up that the deceased had been raised in Dolhinov, White Russia. My ears perked up.

"My grandparents were from Dolhinov," I blurted out.

"Rabbi Ruderman, my father's cousin, is also from Dolhinov," offered the surviving Kaminetsky.

"What? Rabbi Ruderman from Dolhinov?!" I nearly fell off my seat.

"In my day, we all knew that the Rosh Yeshiva had been called in his youth 'Yankel Dolhinover,'" chimed in the elderly Jew from Zichron Yaakov.

"You studied with Rabbi Ruderman all those years and never knew that he was from Dolhinov?" Rabbi Nathan was incredulous.

Quick clarification revealed that the Kaminetskys (unlike the Futterfasses, and the Alperowitzes, my ancestors) had been *misnagdim*, opponents of Hasidism. Rav Yaakov Kaminetsky's father, as my great-grandfather Zalman Mendel, had made his living from the lumber industry in Dolhinov. Logs would be floated down the river Dvinosa for export to Germany. I had heard details of that lumber industry on my Bobbe's knee.

Many times over the years Rav Ruderman had asked me where I was from. Always my answer had been, "Bangor."

Rabbi Shalom Baer Schneersohn (RaSHaB)
[1861-1920]

The Rashab's Hasid

AT THE PULPIT STOOD A LITTLE OLD RABBI WITH A white beard. He had asked permission to say a few words. The few other Jews and I who had gathered in Beth Abraham Synagogue for Sabbath services were totally unprepared for what followed.

His face turning as red as the velvet of the *parochet* (covering of the Ark) behind him, he yelled at the top of his lungs: ***GALEY KEVOD MALCHUSCHO OLEYNU!*** (***"Reveal the glory of Your kingdom to us!"***)

There were titters here and there. He went on in this same impassioned voice to demand of God immediate revelation. My fellow congregants, more at home than I in Yiddish, assumed the man was unbalanced. My own impressions as a teenager were that this was how the Baal Shem Tov might have preached.

This was my first exposure to an honest to goodness Lubavitcher. Nachman Kowalsky had been born to a family of Polish hasidim, adherents of Sochaczew and Gur. In the years immediately preceding World War One, Habad hasidim active in the Polish capital, persuaded the teenager to run away from home to study in Lubavitch, Russia. He returned to Warsaw several years later, a complete convert to Habad.

Since his arrival in this country in the late twenties, Rabbi Nachman Kowalsky had spent most of his years as a *meshulach* (fundraiser) for the Baltimore yeshiva. It seems that he was quite successful, for today the yeshiva occupies a beautiful campus. Students *kibitzed* that Kowalsky's key to success was paying a visit to the local cemetery before descending on a community's philanthropists. By memorizing the information contained on the tombstones, he could pass himself off as an old friend of the family.

He would come every year to collect money from the Etzkovitzes, the potato kings of Aroostook County, and the legendary Striars of Bangor, who had made their money in woolen mills. Misanthropic but lovable Pinny Nissenbaum, who put up all the *meshulochim* in his home, would swear: "The only real rabbi is Rabbi Kowalsky. All the rest are fakers." While on tour, his diet consisted of fruits and vegetables. He never missed

Rabbi Nachman Kowalsky
[1895-1978]

a *tevillah* (ritual immersion). One winter he was arrested by the local police for nudity. It seems he had picked a hole in the ice of the Penobscot. I was enchanted by him and began to follow him around. We spoke in Hebrew, my Yiddish being too poor.

Years later, as a student of Baltimore Yeshiva, I witnessed Kowalsky's pathetic attempt to impart hasidism to the students of the *misnagdic* yeshiva. He transformed what would otherwise have been a tame Friday night Sabbath meal into a crash course in Hasidism.

He started by introducing the man seated next to him at table as a descendant of Reb Michel Zlotchover, disciple of the Baal Shem Tov. He went on to briefly describe the rebirth of hasidism in Israel, from which he had recently returned. He was very impressed by the Gerrer institutions of learning. Then abruptly, or so it seemed, Kowalsky stood up, saying: "I will teach you a *niggun* (hasidic tune) I heard from the Rebbe Rashab many years ago." Within seconds his face assumed that same beet-red hue I had seen in Bangor and he was thumping out an ecstatic Lubavitch tune. He called to the students to join him in song and dance. A couple did, to mock him.

Another Shavuot festival. This time at 770 Eastern Parkway, "World Lubavitch Headquarters." Seated at the dais is the Lubavitcher Rebbe, Menahem Mendel

II. The audience is a crowd of thousands. Of a sudden, I see a big basket of fruits rocking about on the waves of humanity. As the basket approaches my station at the Rebbe's feet, I get a glimpse into the face of its bearer. It is none other than old Rabbi Kowalsky. Having swum all the way up to the Rebbe, he presents him with this gift, invoking the Talmudic dictum: "Nowadays, one who wishes to bring *bikkurim* (first-fruits) to the Temple should offer them as a gift to a sage." The Rebbe instructs him to give the basket of fruits to a certain *kohen* (member of the priestly class descended from Aaron) seated nearby.

My final encounter with Rabbi Kowalsky is on the street outside the building. I introduce myself. He immediately turns that now familiar shade and half yells, half implores: "You must go out to your brothers. How will you enjoy heaven knowing that your brother sits in hell?!"

"The Cave of Machpelah"
Final page of *Shevet Mussar* (Jerusalem, 1863).

A Day in the Court of Menucha Rochel

HAVE YOU EVER GUARDED? GUARD DUTY IS A unique activity. It differs from sleep in that one's eyes are open. As the mind tires from tedium, attention wanders.

I was assigned by the municipality of Kiryat Arba to guard the historic Jewish cemetery in the heart of Hebron. My wife and I—we were in our 20s and yet without children—had exhausted our meager financial resources hiring movers to bring our belongings to the Kirya. I rode in the back of the ancient truck with an Arab mover from Hebron who told me of the fiancee he hoped to bring over from Jordan. Flat broke, I sold my wife's extensive collection of French books and Japanese prints in an improvised open-air market on the campus of Hebrew University in Jerusalem.When the proceeds from the sale ran out, I signed up for guard duty. Rabbi Levinger, unofficial *mukhtar* (Arabic, mayor) of Kiryat Arba, comforted me with a quotation from David's Psalms: "Better a day in Your courts than a thousand in the land of the nations; I chose to stand by the entrance of the house of my God rather than dwell in the tents of wickedness."

So here I am in the Jewish cemetery of Hebron. Most of the old graves have disappeared without a trace after years of Jordanian occupation. One huge tombstone juts out from the otherwise level terrain. It is the (reconstructed) monument of the great mystic Rabbi Elijah De Vidas, author of *Reshit Hokhma* (*Beginning of Wisdom*), deceased some four hundred years. Also preserved are numerous stones from 1929, the year of the infamous Hebron pogrom. At the entrance to the cemetery lies the gravestone of baby Avraham Yedidyah Nachshon, the first Jew to be buried in Hebron since the city was rendered *Judenrein* in the 1930s.

But I feel myself gravitating to a smaller burial ground across the road, that had been reserved for the Habad community of Hebron. There, under piles of debris, lies the legendary Rebbetzin Menucha Rochel, daughter of the *Mitteler Rebbe*, Dov Baer Shneuri. Born on Yud Tes Kislev, the very day of her grandfather's release from the St. Petersburg prison, she was named by him, "Menucha." The *Alter Rebbe* had said, "Now there will be *menucha* (rest)." She and her husband, surnamed Slonim, had settled in Hebron in 1845. Slonim died soon after their arrival in the Holy Land.

Menucha Rochel was the highest ranking hasidic figure in the land at the time and there hung over her a halo of holiness. She had her own study house and *mikveh* (ritual bath) in which she immersed every eve of the Sabbath. Great hasidic rebbes, such as the Shinaver and the Lelover, stood in awe of her.

"Bobbe" Menucha Rochel lived to see the fifth generation. In this plot were buried her descendants, prominent members of the Ashkenazi community. The last Ashkenazic rabbi of Hebron was a Jacob Joseph Slonim. One day I would briefly encounter outside Hadassah Hospital in Hebron a gent by the name of Slonim, who had survived the 1929 massacre. He had been a child at the time. Thinking back, he remarked, "Just from the din of the death chants, you could die of fright."

As I stood towering over what for lack of markers had become a collective grave, I looked out to the Hebron cityscape. I began to glimpse the features of perhaps the most powerful spiritual woman I ever knew, Bessie Motuick (pronounced Motchook).

Bessie and Abe were an old childless couple who lived near the *schule* (synagogue). Their proportions were reminiscent of Laurel and Hardy: Bessie was immense, Abe tiny. Their attire might have been the same set of clothes they wore upon arrival in the New World. Abe's fashion consisted of a nondescript baggy brown suit. Bessie wore an outdated flower print and covered her hair with a round white hat. Abe was proud of his tenor voice; he had sung with a cantor's choir in the Old Country. Bessie had been a nurse in Russia. Eventually they wound up in Winnipeg, Manitoba, where they attached themselves to the Makarover Rebbe. (Makarov is a branch of the Chernobyl-Twersky dynasty.) Later during World War II, they hopped a train to Maine to join relatives. Abe never forgot the antisemitic slurs of the GIs during the long, grueling train ride.

The first years, Abe used to peddle an ointment he developed. He swore to its curative powers. When I knew him, Abe had long since abandoned dreams of making it rich off his wonder drug and looked forward instead to being interred in the Trisker Maggid's *kittel.** Abe's mother had been a devotee of the Trisker, and thus the *kittel* once worn by the Maggid had come into his possession. Every year, Abe faithfully cel-

---

* Trisker Maggid is the title of Rabbi Abraham Twersky (1806-1889), the *maggid* or preacher of Turisk, a third

ebrated the Trisker's *yahrzeit* (annual observance of day of death) with a *kiddush* (an aperitif with religious significance). When the men seated around the table would ask, "Avrohom, whose *yahrzeit* is it?" he would beam, "The Trisker Maggid's." The men would overcome their ignorance with a shot of whiskey and wish, "*Die neshomo zoll hoben an aliyah*" (The soul should have an ascent).

Bessie was another story altogether. She kept her business booming until the day she died. Her business was "viddehs and orphans." Over the years, she singlehandedly raised hundreds of thousands of dollars for the fund she established to aid the widows and orphans of soldiers fallen in Israel's wars.

I remember vividly the day she walked into my grandmother's grocery store. This was no *schnorrer*. She radiated authority. You had to give. There was no choice. Being a child, I could not follow the intricacies of the Yiddish conversation between the two ladies, but the gist was: "You give and in this merit your son will get married." Within no time, my uncle, a confirmed bachelor of several years, was standing under the *huppah* (wedding canopy).

---

generation *rebbe* of the Chernobyl dynasty. The *kittel* is a white robe worn by men on Yom Kippur and at the Passover seder table; it also serves as a burial shroud.

An image of a hospital room comes up. I've just come back from six months of travel. During my spiritual odyssey, I had hitch-hiked thousands of miles. Hearing Bessie is terminally ill, I rush to her bedside. It takes some convincing that it's really her. There lies before me a very thin woman. She speaks to me as if out of a fog. She hands me a letter from the president of Israel thanking her for the latest sum she sent over. (Bessie keeps a couple of Jewish lawyers busy administering the fund.) "Nu, vat you tink of dat, eh?"

She becomes animated, speaking of the *mitsvah* she's doing helping the "viddehs and orphans." By the time I leave, Bessie is back on the phone they've installed next to her bed, calling for—what else?—"de viddehs and orphans."

A few days later I receive a call. It's the *hevrah kadisha* (burial society). Bessie has died. There are no women available to do the *taharah* (the ritual washing of corpse). Would I come down to wash the body?

The call of the *muezzin* blasting from the loud-speakers outside the Cave of Machpelah jolts me back to reality.

Rabbi Moshe Segal
[1904-1985]

The Shofar Blower

HE WAS KNOWN IN JERUSALEM SIMPLY AS THE "*baal tokeya*," the "*shofar* blower." When the British forbade Jews from blowing the *shofar* at the Wailing Wall, he was the young man who had the guts to sound the traditional ram's horn at the conclusion of Yom Kippur. He was promptly imprisoned by the mandatory authorities and subsequently freed only through the personal intervention of Rav Kook, the chief rabbi. Rav Kook threatened not to break his fast until the "offender" was set loose.

When I became acquainted with Rabbi Moshe Segal, he was already an old man, but none of the idealism of youth had left him.

I had been sent by Rav Zevi Yehuda Kook to meet someone at a demonstration at Hakiryah, the seat of Israeli government. The small crowd outside Prime

Minister Begin's office were mostly students of Rav Kook's *yeshiva*, there to protest Begin's ceding Jewish land to surrounding Arab nations. On the platform, spoke a slight man with a white beard. He had about him all the intensity of an Israelite prophet of old. Imagine my surprise when the "prophet" actually began to speak the ancient Hebrew words from the Book of Kings concerning Ahab, King of Israel and Ben Haddad, King of Aram. I never found the person I was supposed to meet, but my encounter with the prophet was more than sufficient reward.

Toward the end of his days, Segal worked as a civil servant in Jerusalem's religious council. His relationship to the office was nothing less than Kafkaesque. The dreamer and fighter for Israel's independence, the ideologist of *Berit ha-Hashmonaim* ("Covenant of the Hasmoneans"), a religious offshoot of Jabotinsky's Revisionist movement, was reduced to politely listening to the idle chatter of his fellow civil servants.

In the privacy of his cubicle, he unburdened himself. Like so many of Israel's pioneers, he had come from Russia. What hadn't he done for his country? He had dried her swamps, paved her roads. But this was a pious pioneer. He had been one of the original founders of Kefar Habad, the Habad village near Lod, in the first years of the state.

His home town of Poltava, as many Russian towns, contained a mixed population of *hasidim* and *mitnagdim*. The rabbi of the hasidic community had been Jacob Mordecai Bezpulov, study companion to the Rebbe Rashab. The *mitnagdim* were led by Rabbi Elijah Akiba Rabinowitz, editor of the anti-Zionist *Ha-Peless*. In his youth, Segal knew Rabbi Hayyim Eliezer Bichovsky, who in the teens published in Poltava several important works of Habad hasidism. Torah Judaism was given a morale boost when, as a result of the upheavals of the First World War, the Mirrer Yeshiva, one of Lithuania's finest Talmudic academies, relocated to Poltava, Ukraine. The earnestness of the students, with whom he became intimately acquainted, made an indelible impression on Segal.

Yes, Segal was a Habadnik, but his love for *Erets Yisrael* came first. He had never seen the Rebbe, unwilling to leave the land for even a visit of such importance. He had seen the previous rebbe, Joseph Isaac, on the latter's pilgrimage to the Holy Land in 1928.

In 1967, right after the capture of the Old City of Jerusalem, he moved in. At first he was a lone Jew sleeping in the rubble of the former Jewish Quarter. His only neighbors were Arabs. Later, other Jews arrived, and today the area throbs with Jewish life.

He was thoroughly disillusioned with Begin. "I

knew something was wrong when he formed a coalition with the Liberals. What has happened is that he is totally caught up in his mythos of peace."

He remonstrated with me to revive the vision, to go out to secular, leftist Israeli youth and implant in them the spirit.

"When I was young, we had none of the vessels but we had the light. Today, we have the vessels, all the trappings of statehood, but we have lost the light."

Moshe Segal was no longer the kinetic youth. Old age had descended upon him and he broke down crying old man's tears.

Fittingly, Moshe Segal passed away on Yom Kippur. As his grandson expressed it, those lungs that had suffered so much sent heavenward their last shrill note, "*Tekiyah!*"

Rabbi Baruch Naeh
[1915-1996]

The Hidden Prince

According to Hasidic lore, there are *zaddikim* (righteous persons) who are revealed and *zaddikim* who are hidden. Rabbi Baruch Naeh was a *nistar*, a hidden one. I first heard of him from the irascible *gaon*, Hayyim Zimmerman. Rabbi Zimmerman was known to cut up the greatest scholars of the generation. It was a backhanded compliment to be singled out for Zimmerman's wrath. Rav Soloveichik, Rav Hutner, Rav Shach—none escaped this man's purview. In this vein, I once heard the sage of Ammunition Hill mention the name "Rav Baruch Naeh." I was intrigued and made a mental note to someday track down this obscure character.

Years later, I was standing on the terrace of my apartment in the Bayit Vegan section of Jerusalem when I observed walking below a man of noble bearing. His beard, white but for a few blond strands of youth, framed a handsome face. His dress was neat, his gait regal. This was Rav Naeh.

He had been pointed out to me a while ago seated at the dais at a gathering organized by Habad to celebrate completing study of Maimonides. Yet no one could tell me where he resided. A search of the telephone directory was in vain. The man left no traces. Neighbors had never heard of him. On several different occasions, he would pass my apartment building. My reaction was always the same. I would watch him, transfixed by his noble rabbinic appearance but powerless to contact him. One day he passed me while I was standing below. I almost summoned the courage to confront him, but experienced failure of nerve when he stared at me harshly. Finally, by following his movements, I discovered that he prayed at the local Sephardic synagogue on Friday evenings.

One Sabbath night after services, I finally cornered him on his way out. I said to him: "I know who you are. You are Rav Naeh." No acknowledgment, only a blink of the eyes. "I want to become your student." A burst of raucous laughter. We proceeded to walk home.

"How did you hear of me?"

"From Rabbi Hayyim Zimmerman."

"Ah. Zimmerman said to me that I would not be an *iluy* (a prodigy) by his uncle Reb Baruch Ber's standards, but that by today's standards I am a genius." He probed my knowledge of Talmud.

"Fine. I have no *talmidim*. A student would have to commit himself for two years just so I could teach him proper methodology in *Tosafot* (commentary to Talmud by medieval French rabbis)."

From that night on, our relationship flourished, and in months to come I became a regular visitor to the Naeh home. Rav Baruch and I resonated well together. On the surface, ours was a scholarly relationship, but underneath was an exchange of souls.

Naeh was the scion of distinguished *halachists*. His grandfather Mendel, from an old Habad family in Hebron, had been a disciple of Rabbi Shlomo Zalman of Lublin and later Jerusalem, author of the volume of responsa, *Torat Hessed*. Baruch's father was Rav Avraham Hayyim Naeh, the nemesis of the famed "Hazon Ish" regarding Torah measurements. The *yeshiva* world has opted for the sage of B'nai Berak, "Hazon Ish", by and large, but in Jerusalem circles the elder Naeh was esteemed more highly. While yet a very young man, Avraham Hayyim had been invited by the Rebbe Rashab to head his *yeshiva* in Lubavitch, Russia. The son, Baruch, took umbrage against his father's opponents and remained a quixotic figure ready to fight at a moment's notice. His father's legal decisions were considered authoritative and binding by the

Lubavitcher Rebbe. Rav Baruch himself every year put out the official Lubavitch synagogue calendar replete with halachic dicta. It was truly a privilege to be exposed to this last of a species, the Habad *halachist*.

A few days before Passover, 1987, I am to fly to America. I knock on Rav Baruch's door, both to ask him intricate *halachic* questions regarding the holiday and also to take leave of him. His mind, despite his many illnesses and hospitalizations, is razor sharp. His answers are lucid and brilliant. He tells me how to dispose of the *hamets* (leavened bread forbidden on Passover) in this case complicated by time zones, and how to observe the second days of *yom tov* in the Diaspora.

"The *Shaar ha-Kollel* did not understand the *Alter Rebbe*'s reasoning. There is no mysticism here. Rav Zalman's ruling is based on Rabbenu Hananel in the Tractate *Pesahim*." And he shows me the precise passage in the Babylonian *Talmud*.

Rav Naeh hands me a memento, a book of his father's he published.

We are now on the landing. My mentor and friend squeezes my hand. "I love *Erets Yisrael*," he says a few times as tears well up in his eyes. "I once had to spend two years in America. Once aboard the ship to Israel, I looked back at the American shore and uttered a prayer, 'Lord, please, I never want to see that land again.'"

"But I am only going to the States for a couple of weeks."

Silence.

How did Rav Naeh know that a visit of a few weeks would develop into a stay of several, several years?

The Kabbalist

I DISCOVERED HIM ON A VISIT TO THE *YESHIVA* OF Rabbi Moshe Feinstein, Tifereth Jerusalem, on the Lower East Side. What immediately struck one was his disheveled appearance, hat askew, and pipe jutting out of his mouth. We must have been about the same age, but invisible worlds set us apart.

It is my suspicion that he was the only authentic kabbalist America ever produced. He was introduced to the esoteric lore at a tender age by his grandfather, a Lubavitcher from the Old Country.

If poetry is any indication of what one human feels for another, I would say he admired me, for he once composed a Hebrew poem in my honor.

He took me to his home where he lit *yahrzeit* candles for the righteous who had passed on. The atmosphere was absolutely eery.

As we walked the streets of the rundown Lower East Side, he asked me if I knew the difference between *merirut* (bitterness) and *atsvut* (sadness). According to the *Tanya*, bitterness is positive, for remorse can bring to arousal and repentance, whereas depression stems from *kelipah*, impurity and stops up the heart. I could not fathom to what he was alluding.

He told me that in America there were only two men truly adept in the intricacies of the Kabbalah, the Lubavitcher Rebbe and the Skolyer Rebbe. He would discuss Kabbalah with these two venerable sages on intimate terms.

We made up to meet at the Skolyer Rebbe's residence, in Brooklyn. He would be my entree to the Rebbe.

I was there at the appointed time. I had taken the liberty of inviting a close friend, Michael. Michael showed. The two of us waited for the kabbalist. He was nowhere in sight. Meanwhile the Skolyer Rebbe's *gabbai* (attendant) heard two voices below his window and buzzed us in. We were not granted admission to the Rebbe, but as a consolation, the *gabbai* offered me all the Rebbe's books. Later, I spoke to the kabbalist by phone. He had gotten lost in the subway system.

On my next visit to New York, I placed a call to the kabbalist. His father answered. He began to grill me. "What is your name?" "How do you know my son?" "No, you can't speak to him." "The next time you are in the vacinity come by and I will discuss with you."

Why was I being subjected to interrogation?

Years later, I bumped into an acquaintance from the Lower East Side. He told me the following story: The youthful kabbalist had thrown himself into the East River. Though normally Jewish Law denies all honors to suicides, since the deceased was under psychiatric care, the preeminent decisor of *halacha*, Rabbi Moshe Feinstein had paid homage to the young man by eulogizing him.

The kabbalist had crossed the thin line between *merirut* (remorse) and *atsvut* (depression).

Rabbi Shlomo Carlebach
[1925-1994]

The Master of Prayer

Rabbi Nachman of Braslav told the tale of a *baal tefillah* (master of prayer) who lived outside of civilization and would make periodic forays into society to pluck out souls. Having charmed these individuals with his song, he would then return with them to his hideout. Eventually, he won over the entire nation. In our generation there lived such a master of song. His name was Shlomo Carlebach.

The Carlebach family, which traces its lineage back to the TaZ,* produced some of the most prominent rabbis in Germany. Shlomo's youth was spent in

* Rabbi David Halevy (circa 1586-1667), known as "TaZ," acronym of *Turei Zahav*, his commentary to the *Shulhan Arukh*.

Vienna between the two world wars. The ship which carried him to safety was the last to leave Europe for the United States. Acknowledged as an *iluy*, a prodigy, he experienced a meteoric rise to fame in the *yeshiva* world, first in Rabbi Isaac Hutner's Yeshiva Rabbi Chayim Berlin and later in Rabbi Aaron Kotler's Lakewood Yeshiva. Rabbi Kotler had high hopes for Shlomo. When Shlomo later came under the influence of Joseph Isaac of Lubavitch, this only exacerbated Reb Aaron's contempt for Lubavitch.

Rabbi Aaron Kotler, doyen of the Lithuanian *roshei yeshivos*, declared a holy war on Lubavitch. Certainly, the underlying issues ran deep, but the straw which broke the camel's back was Joseph Isaac's interpretation of the four categories of damages at the beginning of Tractate *Bava Kamma*—"the ox, the pit, the tooth and the fire"—as four evil spirits. Such reifying of Talmudic learning was anathema to the Lithuanian talmudist sworn to up-hold in its purity the tradition of the Vilna Gaon.

Rabbi Joseph Isaac had enormous impact on the impressionable young Carlebach. He convinced him to go out to his brothers and sisters to bring errant souls back to their source. The key to their hearts would be music.

As time went on, Shlomo moved farther and farther away from the talmudism of the *yeshiva* world and increasingly into the world of Hasidism and music. His road to stardom commenced in a cafe in the Village.

There was a time when Shlomo still attempted to straddle the fence. He was walking down the street in Manhattan with two Lakewood *roshei yeshivos.* Suddenly he heard someone call in a sort of drawl: "Shlomoe!" Across the street was a renowned female black recording artist. He buried his head hoping the voice would disappear. It persisted. Again, "Shloe-moe!" He buried his head even deeper. Finally the voice yelled out: "Shloe-moe, you - - - - - - - - - - - - - !" By this time, Shlomo's nose was a centimeter above the sidewalk.

Judith Malina, co-founder of The Living Theatre, made Shlomo's acquaintance in his father Rabbi Naphtali's synagogue. In a 1956 entry to her Diary, she portrayed thus the 30-year old Carlebach:

> This Shlomo is a modern intellectual under his bushy, dark brown beard, a sophisticated chassid who has struck out a singular path for himself.
>
> I like his fervor.
>
> Only age can fulfill his desire, and waiting is hard. But a good doctrine has been given to him and he has not forsaken it.

Eventually, Shlomo outgrew Lubavitch as well.

Come the sixties, Rabbi Shlomo Carlebach was spiritual leader to the "flower children," with headquarters in the House of Love and Prayer in San Francisco. This was a new Shlomo, different from the apprentice to either Aaron Kotler or Joseph Isaac Schneersohn: long-haired, sporting a folk singer's vest, and speaking an amalgam of Hippie and Yiddish, in which expressions such as "holy brother," "so-o-o deep," "gevaldig" and "mamash" would alternate with equal frequency.

Shlomo developed his own inimitable way of doing things. For example, the *bedekken* ceremony became the "signature" of a Carlebach wedding. The *bedekken*, where the groom covers the bride's face with the veil—usually over in a few minutes—Shlomo extended to an hour and a half, during which he would give his mystic interpretation of the procedure. Reb Shlomo explained that this was a time for the couple to get back to the origin of their souls, even to Creation itself. The world was created with ten sayings, ten divine fiats. *Bereshit*, "In the beginning," is also a saying, but it is a hidden saying, a saying without words. So the bride is silent. She is also veiled, because as the holy Kotzker pointed out, faith is higher than sight, believing takes one beyond seeing. At the end of the veiling ceremony, it is customary for the groom (and his male entourage) to dance backwards away from the bride—back to the origin, to the Beginning.

In the seventies, the center of Shlomo's energy shifted from San Francisco to Me'or Modi'im, the *moshav* (cooperative village or commune) he founded in Israel. In the eighties and nineties, Shlomo would make a comeback in the Manhattan where he had started out. The Carlebach Shul at West 79th Street became a spiritual haven to Jews from all walks of life and of different persuasions. There, West Side sophisticates would meet distinctively garbed hasidic types from Brooklyn's ghettos. All would thrill to the song-and-dance of this spiritual phenomenon. Between sensitive soul-songs, Shlomo would tell hasidic tales.

Perhaps the greatest tribute to Shlomo's mastery of the art of prayer is the fact that my own father, whose immune system since youth produced synagogal antibodies, walked away from Shlomo's *davvenen* (praying) at the Wall with a new appreciation for the beauty of prayer.

The night before Carlebach's funeral I tossed and turned in my sleep. I saw so many different things. They came so fast and so furious. Upon waking, desperate for direction, I consult my Bible. It opens to the passage in Daniel where King Nebuchadnezzar has dreamt bizarre visions which he is at a loss to decipher. He turns to Daniel to interpret the dreams. The reading is a mirror image of my dilemma. So much for oracles!

I call up an unusual scholar whom I consult when I can't tackle a dilemma on my own. His wife informs me he is in Jerusalem for his father's *yahrzeit*.

Alone I drive to the funeral. The long stretch of parkway provides ample opportunity for reflection. Just some months before, Shlomo had been invited to a local synagogue for the Sabbath. The rabbi of the synagogue stood on the sidelines as Carlebach turned the normally reserved service into a veritable *Simhat Torah* (Rejoicing of the Law). Of a sudden, Jews formed ecstatic dance circles enveloping the Torah.

On that occasion, I made a mental note that perhaps not since the Sabbath of Shabbetai Zevi's "coronation" in Izmir in 1666, had there been such a bouleversement. He too was capable of infecting Jews of every stripe with his enthusiasm. According to the chronicler Leib ben Ozer of Amsterdam, the venerable leader of Polish Jewry, Rabbi David Halevy, known as "TaZ," sent his son and stepson to Turkey to investigate the self-proclaimed Messiah. By this time, poor Shabbetai Zevi was already imprisoned in Gallipoli fortress. Once Rabbi Isaiah and Rabbi Aryeh Leib gained admittance to the fortress, they were amazed at what they saw. A robust Shabbetai Zevi was dancing to and fro in his "gilded cage," singing at the top of his lungs the Psalms of David. But to the Sefardic masses of the Levant, the siren song of Shabbetai Zevi was a

Spanish *romanza*, "Meliselda," about the daughter of the King. Shabbetai Zevi read mystic significance into the love song. Needless to say, the Polish emissaries were so captivated by the "Messiah"'s comportment that they returned to the TaZ an unqualifiedly positive report. Unfortunately, within months, the Messiah of Izmir was forcibly converted to Islam.

Outside the Carlebach Shul, the crowd is a cross-section of the Jewish People: Lithuanian talmudists, Hasidim, Sefardim, modern cosmopolitans, unre-formed hippies. Prominent rabbis eulogize the de-ceased singer. A cup is passed around for donations "to bury Reb Shlomo." The hearse wends its way slowly onto the West Side Highway, escorted by Carlebach hasidim humming one of the master's earliest compositions, *Lulay toratkha shaashuai* ("If Your Torah had not been my delight, then I would have been lost in my affliction"), a mournful tune remarkably appropriate as a funeral dirge. To bury Reb Shlomo in Israel.

The New Age Rebbe

A FRIEND WAS DESCRIBING A RETREAT OF RURAL Jewish communities that he and his family had attended in Vermont.

"There was a Lubavitch rabbi there who wore some kind of white robe Friday night."

I quickly corrected him. Lubavitcher rabbis wear black, not white, frock coats.

My friend insisted that the rabbi had identified himself as Lubavitch-trained. Suddenly it dawned on me whom he was describing.

"Was his name perhaps Shneur?"

"Yes, that's it. Reb Shneur."

Reb Shneur is the rebbe of the New Age movement. On this particular occasion, he had worn white robes. On other occasions, he has been known to sport a rainbow-colored *tallit*. Though it has been several decades since he officially represented the Lubavitch movement, his involvement with Habad is no hoax. The history of Habad in America must include Reb Shneur just as the Talmud encompasses the maverick Elisha ben Abuyah—subject of Milton Steinberg's novel *As a Driven Leaf*—and as the hasidic chronicles mention an unnamed "Rabbi of Volpa," who began as the star pupil of the Maggid of Mezritch and ended as an "alcoholic vagabond."

As many natives of the former Austrian territory of Galicia, Shneur's family lived between the two world wars in Vienna. With the nazification of Austria, they fled to Belgium. There, the teenage Shneur had his first taste of Habad hasidism. He joined a group studying *Tanya* under the direction of a Reb Moshe, *mashgiah* of the *yeshiva* in Heide near Antwerp. Moshe Tchechowal,* hailed from Kishinev and had been a disciple of the Rav of Kishinev, Rabbi Judah Leib Zirelsohn, and of Rabbi Abraham Schneersohn, father-

---

* Editor's note: According to the research of David Kranzler and Eliezer Gevirtz, a Rabbi Mosco Czechoval and his group of 300 Orthodox Jews survived the War and were transferred from Italy to Fort Ontario near Oswego, New York. See D. Kranzler and E. Gevirtz, *To Save a World*, Vol. II (New York: CIS, 1991), pp. 126-27.

in-law of the sixth Lubavitcher Rebbe, Joseph Isaac.

During this twilight period on the eve of destruction, the young Shneur also made the acquaintance of the man who some ten years later would head the Lubavitch movement, Menahem Mendel Schneerson (son-in-law of Joseph Isaac). Menahem Mendel at this time kept a very low profile, but Shneur distinctly remembers him delivering a talk to a group of Lubavitch *talmidim*. He interpreted the first *mishnah* in Tractate *Ketubot* in a kabbalistic vein. "A virgin is married on the fourth day (of the week) and a widow on the fifth day," says the Mishnah. According to the future Lubavitcher Rebbe, the fourth day refers to the fourth millenium and the fifth day to the fifth millenium. The woman represents the Jewish People, which is to be married to God. Ideally, the union would have occurred during the virginity of the Jewish People in the fourth millennium. Now it must take place during our widowhood in the fifth millenium since creation. He concluded his talk by crying, "When will it be already?"

Arriving in New York at the onset of World War II, Shneur continued his studies in the Lubavitch Yeshiva. Eventually he was sent out by the Rebbe as an emissary to bring Jews back to the fold. In 1949, at Rabbi Joseph Isaac's behest, he set out to influence students at Brandeis University. His first pulpit was a small Massachusetts community. Later, he was active in a city in western Canada.

Ever seeking to expand his horizons, he went through several different phases. During his spiritualist stage, roughly a year after the passing of Rabbi Joseph Isaac Schneersohn in 1950, Shneur consulted a woman medium (though contacting the spirit world may be problematic from a point of view of Jewish law). The Anglican spiritualist reported that she saw a man wearing a big sable fur hat, with a beautiful beard and awesome to behold, coming down from the twentieth plane! "He was your master in this life."

In his New England period, he experimented with setting English lyrics to time-honored Hasidic *niggunim*. To Reb Michel Zlotchover's *niggun* he wrote these words:

> I came to my garden from beyond time and space
> To meet my bride, my beloved at our own special
>   meeting place
> For not the angels of heaven above
> But you my Jews I love
> My Lord, my love, my groom
> With thee let me commune . . . .

His attempts at outreach spurred him to develop novel methods. By the late fifties he was teaching meditation to Hillel members on campus. With the passage of time he became increasingly disaffected with

Habad's overemphasis on the cerebral to the neglect of the emotional, imaginative and sensual dimensions of spirituality. His father being a Galician hasid, he rediscovered more holistic forms of Hasidism in Bobov, Braslav and Reb Arele Roth of Satu-Mare and Jerusalem.

A critical turning point was an LSD trip in the sixties with Dr. Timothy Leary, the Harvard psychologist.

It became apparent to Shneur that God is not Jewish, the universe is not Jewish, but Sinai is Jews' way of hooking into the cosmos. The vastness of it all led Shneur to venture beyond Judaism to explore other religions: Christianity, Hinduism, Islam, the ancient Canaanite pantheon. The break with Lubavitch, long in coming, was inevitable.

When Dr. Trude Weiss-Rosmarin, editor of the *Jewish Spectator*, attacked him in her paper for having taken LSD with Leary, Shneur was crestfallen that the Lubavitch movement did not come to his defense.

Once asked if he is a lost soul, Shneur's initial reaction was a rendition of "Amazing Grace" ("I once was lost but now I'm found"). In a more serious vein, he continued: "I don't feel lost but there are times I would like to be around a *tisch* (literally, "table," a hasidic gathering). Yud Tes Kislev, for example. But Lubavitch is not my home anymore . . ."

Rabbi Shlomo Twersky
[1923-1981]

Sound of Silence

I HAD SAT OPPOSITE THIS MAN FOR ABOUT AN HOUR, during which time he had expressed all of two thoughts, both uttered with extreme brevity. I had come hoping for enlightenment. Honestly, I found his silence maddening. This was not a Freudian therapist, but a hasidic *rebbe*, Shlomo Twersky, the so-called "Denver Rebbe." (The two thoughts I heard on that occasion were his disapproval of Gershom Scholem's books on Kabbalah and his advice to study *Shulhan Arukh*, the *Code of Jewish Law*.)

His spartan appearance matched perfectly his taciturnity. A severe black sweater hug his small frame, while coal like eyes dominated his gaunt face. Tired of the spiritual exercise of riding New York's subways, I toyed with the idea of relocating to the Rockies. The Denver Rebbe held out no hope. If anything, he gave me to understand that nothing real would be accomplished by the move.

Rabbi Twersky was the scion of the Hornosteipel dynasty, which may be conceptualized as an amalgam of Chernobyl and Lubavitch. His ancestor, Mordecai Dov of Hornosteipel, was named after two great-grandfathers, Mordecai of Chernobyl and Dov Baer of Lubavitch. (Mordecai's son, Jacob Israel Twersky of Tcherkass, had married the daughter of Dov Baer Shneuri, the *Mitteler Rebbe*.) Because of the pervasive Habad influence, the Hornosteipelers had been viewed as the "black sheep" of the Twersky family. The Denver Rebbe continued this allegiance to and stress upon study of *Tanya*. He was striving very much, in the footsteps of *Tanya*, to translate kabbalistic themes of Isaac Luria to psychology. One such recorded talk of his is an attempt to make the arcane terms *Ibbur*, *Yenikah*, *Mohin* (Gestation, Nursing, Brains) come alive.

Born in Cracow in 1923, Shlomo arrived in this country as a child. His father, who served as spiritual shepherd to a flock of Russian and Ukrainian immigrants in Milwaukee, was one of the relatively few hasidic *rebbes* in the United States prior to World War II.

The Denver Rebbe's audience was by-and-large *baalei teshuvah*, individuals from mostly secular families who had warmed to Hasidism. Shlomo

Twersky himself, it seems, was a man in rebellion. He had shaken up or down (I'm not sure which) the glatt kosher meat industry by exposing "shortcuts" taken to streamline mass production. Eventually, he set up his own slaughterhouse where the ritual laws were scrupulously observed. Beyond that, his congregation of "hippies" did not exactly endear him to his Orthodox rabbinic colleagues, be they mithnagdic or hasidic. It would be a mistake to assume that brilliance paves the road to success. More often than not, a prodigious mind creates more problems than it solves. Shlomo Twersky had been an *iluy*, a child prodigy. At age seventeen he knew Hayyim Vital's kabbalistic manual *Peri Ets Hayyim* (*Fruit of the Tree of Life*) backwards and forwards. For his restless, searching mind, he paid a heavy price.

Intellectually, he was exploring uncharted lands. He dared to fuse the *Tanya* of his ancestor together with the teachings of the earlier Italian mystic, Rabbi Moshe Hayyim Luzzatto.

One of Rabbi Twersky's most important teachings was to be "grounded." Father Jacob's vision was of a ladder standing upon the ground and reaching for heaven. In the Hebrew original, the ladder does not yet touch earth; it extends toward the earth (*artsah*). Rabbi Twersky taught that earth too—not only heaven—is a goal to be striven for.

His end, a premature end, came on *Simhat Torah*, the day of the Rejoicing of the Law, perhaps the happiest day of the year. He instructed his disciples not to visit him in the hospital, rather spend the day as every year, dancing with the Torah scrolls in the synagogue. As the hasidim, a most unconventional group of hasidim, danced to the heavens, unbeknown to them, the lonely dance of their beloved rebbe reached much higher—and also lower.

Chaos Theory

I WAS SITTING IN MY STUDY, INSIDE THE BOMB SHELTER we had converted into a *kollel* for advanced rabbinic studies. Over the years in Kiryat Arba, I had graduated from guardsman to head of this institution of higher learning. In walked David Ben-Yosef, author of a minor best-seller, *Is There a Chance for Love*? On the cover of Ben-Yosef's book was a picture of a peaceful stream, beautiful flowers, and a bust of the Lubavitcher Rebbe, drawn by the author's friend, the artist Baruch Nachshon. In the book, Ben-Yosef confronts the pain and pleasure of life.

Ben-Yosef ran the local *kupat holim* or health clinic. He was the exact opposite of a bureaucrat. He took such an interest in each patient that just exposure to his words was half a healing. When we left for the United States, he imparted to my wife these words:

"Jacob, on his way into exile, dreamt angels ascending and descending. The angels are the Jewish People themselves. Sometimes Jews go up to the Land; other times they go down from the Land. But they are still angels."

It would be hard to find someone more individualistic than David Ben-Yosef. I can still see him dancing barefoot on the floor of Nachshon's living room during Sabbath morning prayers, his arms gracefully stroking the air. Were these movements of modern interpretive dance or was he attempting to retrace the dance steps of his namesake King David?

He has come to the "bunker" on an urgent mission. He is on his way to Tel-Aviv to meet with nationally famous novelist Dan Ben-Amotz, the trendsetter of Israeli bohemia. But first he needs an hour of my time. Unbeknown to me, I hold the key to Ben-Amotz's heart.

Ben-Yosef wants me to explain to him the significance of Rav Kook's piece, "The Souls of the World of Chaos." Ben-Yosef believes that this is the way home for Dan Ben-Amotz. Deep inside this body so polluted, there lives the soul of a *Tehillim-zogger* (Psalm-sayer), Ben-Amotz's former Yiddish name.

I do my best to explain the scholarly underpinnings of Rav Kook's essay. The concept of *neshamot de-tohu*, "chaotic souls," originates in Lurianic

Kabbalah; later it was expanded in Habad Hasidism. There are souls from a time or world that preceded our own. They are disdainful of this world and its laws because inwardly they yet recall a world much higher. These are the impatient idealists, the great anarchists and revolutionaries.

The *Mitteler Rebbe* holds up as prototypes of *Tohu* (Chaos) and *Tikkun* (Harmony) the twins Esau and Jacob. When the wholly righteous Jacob succeeds in appropriating some of the chaos within his recalcitrant brother Esau's soul, he (Jacob) thereby rises to a level higher than he could otherwise have reached.

I can see my talk going over Ben-Yosef's head. I offer my grandfather's homespun wisdom. Zeide had been the lay leader of a large Jewish community. He had seen the full cycle of life, watched children grow to maturity. He observed to me that those who had been tame in their youth, most times grew up to be mediocre adults; the youngsters who were wild and unruly, invariably emerged as the leaders of the next generation.

I hit home. Ben-Yosef now knew what message to deliver to the *rebbe* of the World of Chaos.

The Forest Dweller

HIS GRANDFATHER, *DER ALTER* (THE ELDER) OF Novahrodok, had lived in isolation in the woods for several years. A meeting with Israel Salanter, the founder of the *Mussar* (Ethical) movement, had transformed the householder into a master of introspection. He dropped his business affairs, bade his family farewell and headed for a remote cabin. As *Rosh Hashanah*, the New Year, approached, the rabbi of Kovno brought every pressure to bear on him to pray with the community in synagogue—to no avail. An immovable Yosef Yozel Hurvitz sounded the *shofar* (ram's horn) from his sylvan seclusion. Eventually, he did emerge from his *hitbodedut* (solitude) to found a *yeshiva* in the city of Novahrodok (Russian, Novogrudok) which would become renowned for the spiritual radicalism of its students. *Der Alter* steeled them to the point where neither social ostracism nor physical danger could make a dent in their conviction.

Hurvitz passed away in 1919. His son-in-law, Abraham Jofen succeeded him. Novahrodok courage stood his disciples in good stead when finally the decision was made to quit Russia for Poland. Originally, the Novahrodokers had thought to confront Bolshevik reality head on, but the saintly *Hafets Hayyim* counseled flight. The young students demonstrated their bravery and ingenuity in surmounting the border controls that had turned the Eurasian colossus into one big prison. Once free, the hardy *mussarniks* immediately set up a network of *yeshivot* that thrived in the Polish republic until the outbreak of World War II. The *rosh yeshiva*, Rabbi Jofen, and his family survived the war to establish Novahrodok in yet another exile: Brooklyn.

Zalman Jofen had been the rebel of the family. He broke away from his strict upbringing to carve out a career for himself as an avantgarde film-maker. His neighbors on Manhattan's East Side included beat poet Allen Ginsberg.

The old man I met one memorable evening in a poorly lit Brooklyn apartment had the gaunt appearance of an inveterate smoker. A mustache loomed large on his face. The prodigal son had returned to his roots—well not quite. The Lubavitcher hasidim had brought him to live in their Crown Heights community. Zalman had found balm for his spirit in the world of hasidism, so very different from his *mitnagdic* patrimony.

I questioned him about that. He told me, the Rebbe is a great man. I had the gall to say:

"Zalman, you see the Rebbe and his court through the eyes of a film-maker." (Zalman had made a film of Lubavitch.)

"My brother who is a *gaon* (Talmudic genius) says the Rebbe is a great scholar."

Zalman's brother, Rabbi Jacob Jofen, the third generation head of the Novahrodok Yeshiva, had a reputation as being expert in the Jerusalem Talmud.

My host shared with me a printed thought of his late father. But the highlight of the evening was when Zalman sang for me from the depths of a soul that had lived much in many different spheres, the song of the Kalever Rebbe.

Yizhak Eizik of Kalev had been the first to spread Hasidism in Hungary. He would listen to the songs of Hungarian shepherds, then convert them to hasidic tunes. This particular tune concerns a flower tucked away in the heart of a forest. To the imagination of the Kalever, the rose suggested the *Shekhinah*, the Divine

Presence, while the immensity of the forest became symbolic of the length of the *Galut*, the Exile.

Forest, forest, how vast you are!
Rose, rose, how far you are!

If the forest was not so vast,
The rose would not be so far.

Exile, exile, how long you are!
Shekhinah, Shekhinah, how distant you are!

If the exile was not so long,
The *Shekhinah* would not be so distant.

Come to think of it, Zalman was too weak to sing for me. He played a recording of himself singing.

Forest had met forest.

In Search of a Soul

I WAS TRAVELING FROM CITY TO CITY. MY MISSION WAS to peddle a softcover brochure on Maimonides' philosophy. The publication, xerox copy with spiral binding, was intended to demonstrate a new methodology of interpreting Maimonides, one which would fuse the analytic and mystic approaches. Or at least, that was my official cover.

Was there any more to this wanderlust? Wandering, "*pravven golus*," is a mystic exercise. The great kabbalists of old would leave their homes for years at a stretch in imitation of the *Shekhinah*'s exile. In my own mind, I would give the Almighty a helping hand in his work of coupling. If it was meant for two particles to collide, I would accelerate the process by increasing the randomness.

When I descended the bus in New York's Port

Authority terminal, I bumped into a *yeshiva* student roughly my age who seemed a candidate likely to purchase my wares. After distractedly perusing the contents, he reached in his pocket and handed me the dollar I was asking for the booklet. We got to talking. It turned out he was enrolled in the Lubavitch Yeshiva in Crown Heights. His vocation in life was to be an artist. The Rebbe had instructed him to study one more year in the *yeshiva* before heading to Les Beaux Arts in Paris. The way he intoned "Beaux Arts," it might have been Shangri-la.

A few years later I again ran into the young artist, this time in a subway station. I was shocked by his transformation. He had shed the traditional hasidic garb and was now dressed as any inhabitant of the Village. More disturbing, his former innocence had been replaced by a biting cynicism. I could feel the gaping wound, the global hurt. He had now become a "dadaist," or so he said. (The little I knew of art history led me to suspect the term was anachronistic.) His new technique of painting consisted of vomiting onto the canvas. (Actually, why go to the bother of converting visceral emotions to the medium of paint, when this way is so much more direct?) He read me a poem he had composed, equally nihilistic in tone. What had happened to the sweet *yeshiva bochur* to anger him so?

I invited him to a class in Maimonides' philosophy I was to give in a synagogue in Brooklyn the following evening. Incredibly, he came. Was he, despite his ostensible rejection of tradition, ever the *habadnik* or incurable intellectual? Of course, after the lecture he told me I had gotten Maimonides all wrong. It occurred to me he was a helium balloon about to sail off; the ribbon to the balloon was fast slipping through my fingers.

Months later, our paths again crossed in New York's bowels. He bade me farewell. His process of self-exploration would now take him to the Amazon Jungle. He had learned from the eminent anthropologist, Michael Harner of the New School for Social Research, of an elixir, *yahe* or *ayahuasca*, from a South American vine. The indigenous tribes employ it in their religious rituals.

"What is so great about this drug?"

"You die."

"What?"

"It simulates the death experience."

My friend had written the Lubavitcher Rebbe a letter informing him he was about to embark for the *selva* and asking him if their was any *shelihut* or mission the Rebbe wanted carried out there.

Years would pass. I myself did some extensive traveling, which took me to other regions. On a foray into New York, for many years my home base, but no longer, I walked into 770 Eastern Parkway, "World Lubavitch Headquarters." It was already past noon. The men were just finishing morning prayers. (Lubavitchers pray late into the day, a shock to outsiders.) One young man tarried after the others. Immersed in prayer, his *tefillin* (phylacteries) appearing massive on his head tonsured hasidic-style, there shone from him an ethereal light. It was him.

He had gotten lost in the jungle. The natives discovered him nearly dead and nursed him back to health. He never got to ingest the wonder drug.

The last I heard, my young friend is an accomplished professor of Jewish Thought at a prominent institution.

Rabbi Menahem Mendel Schneersohn I
[1789-1866]

An Andean Interlude

MY THIRST FOR RARE OUT-OF-PRINT BOOKS LED ME to the home of Rabbi Mendel Zuber. Someone thought he might possess a copy of Rabbi Eizik of Homel's hasidic work, *Hannah Ariel.*

As I entered the home, I spied hanging under glass on the right hand wall a handwritten page. My host explained that the manuscript bore the signature of the *Zemah Zedek*, Rabbi Menahem Mendel of Lubavitch. He then led me down the stairs to the basement where he stored the volumes of his deceased father's library. Israel Zuber, a graduate of the Lubavitch Yeshiva in Russia, had served as both rabbi and ritual slaughterer in Stockholm. The elder Zuber had been a scholar of some note. In his day, he had exchanged letters with Rabbi Joseph Rosen, the "Rogatchover *Iluy*." It has even been said that at one time

Rabbi Joseph Isaac Schneersohn considered Rabbi Israel Zuber for the job of *rosh yeshiva* of Lubavitch in Brooklyn. Unfortunately, Rabbi Zuber met an untimely death, murdered walking through a Boston park. Mendel showed me one of his most treasured possessions, his father's copy of *Tanya*, margins filled with learned notes.

A volume of Israel Zuber's writings, published posthumously in Israel, contains important discussions by the *halakhic* authorities of the generation concerning the question of electroshocking or stunning the animal before ritual slaughter. The wave of anti-*shehitah* legislation in the thirties, direct outcome of the spread of antisemitism, prompted Rabbi Zuber to submit this *she'elah* (question of Jewish law) before the eminent decisors.

Browsing through the stacks of books, I could not help but notice on the desk a photo of Mendel or Myron surrounded by a group of swarthy youngsters. My quizzical look was enough for Myron to launch into the telling of his missionary activities in Peru.

According to Myron's version, Rabbi Chodakov, the Rebbe's secretary, had entrusted him with the unofficial mission of teaching Judaism to a group of potential converts in Peru. Before Rabbi Myron set out for the Andean highlands, he received from the Lubavitcher Rebbe not one but two dollars, an index of the Rebbe's concern for the *gerim* (converts).

These modern-day descendants of the ancient indigenous races, reside in two communities in northern Peru, one more isolated than the other. One group has set up its own village, Milagro ("Miracle") in the desert outside the coastal town of Trujillo. The second group resides high up in the Andes in remote Cajamarca, famous as the summer resort where Francisco Pizarro captured unawares the Inca emperor Atahualpa. The Milagro group had practically set up their own "Jewish" township. They lived in very primitive conditions: no running water or electricity. They preferred their autonomy to these blandishments of civilization.

All these are the followers of one Segundo Villanueva who, after years of comparative study of the world's major religions, came to the conclusion that Judaism is the way. In anticipation of their actual formal conversion to Judaism, they practiced the commandments at great personal sacrifice. It was not easy for the poor indigens to break out of the mold of the conquistador's Christianity. They eat no meat, recite daily prayers in the Jewish fashion, and on Saturdays the entire community congregate in their makeshift "synagogue" to pray and study the Bible. The men undergo ritual circumcision.

I heard a tape of their original compositions:

Hebrew Psalms set to Andean tunes reminiscent of *El Condor Pasa*. It seems Villanueva's daughter, Eva, was a talented musician.

Just about this time, stories began to circulate in the press about Marrano descendants discovered in New Mexico, but Zuber was convinced his Peruvian students were Inca in origin, not Spanish *conversos*.

When Zuber began to operate in Peru, the dreaded Shining Path (*El Sendero Luminoso*) controlled a good portion of the Peruvian countryside. These were armed Maoists under the direction of former university professor of philosophy Abimael Guzman, in whose catechism human society resembles an ant colony. Zuber related how at gunpoint he was once pulled off a bus travelling through a rural area dominated by the guerillas.

"What did you do?"

"They were looking for North American tourists. The rebel leader, thumbing through my passport, asked me where Sweden is."

"What did you say?"

"*Al lado de Rusia*" (Adjacent to Russia).

"A smile passed over the revolutionary's face."

An Angel

A FRIEND AND I WERE SITTING IN A DAIRY RESTAURANT on Kingston Avenue in Crown Heights, around the corner from "770" (Eastern Parkway), World Lubavitch Headquarters. Seated at the next table was an elderly hasidic gent with an Old World appearance: round beaver hat, *payos* (side curls) wound around the ears, long frock, white socks. He appeared a kindly grandfather. Uninvited, he joined our conversation. His theme was endism. The imminent end of the world was visible in the breakdown of morality and the proliferation of drugs and crime. Our interlocutor invoked the authority of the Maharal of Prague who explains that in order for a new messianic era to commence, it is a logical necessity that the old world order crack. At that point, it dawned on me that the man's outer appearance understated a remarkable complexity.

The conversation wound up with the intruder offering me his telephone number and inviting me to his home for the Sabbath. A single alone in New York City does not sniff at such an offer.

Zanvil Gertner was as good as his word. A telephone call landed me an invitation to his Monsey home. It was winter and the alpine atmosphere of upstate Rockland County intensified the cold. In the few minutes left before Friday night Sabbath prayers, Gertner's son shared with me his worldview: The Rebbe of Satmar, Rabbi Joel Teitelbaum, was the greatest living sage. Anyone else I might have heard of, whether the Skulener or the Ribnitzer or even Reb Itzikel of Antwerp, was second class by comparison.

At the Chentzkovitzer *shtiebel* (hasidic synagogue) next door, I was introduced after the prayer to Steve Hill of *Mission Impossible* fame, a television star recently turned to practicing Judaism.

My host spoke very little during the Sabbath. His only departure from a self-imposed silence was to impart a teaching from the favorite Hungarian hasidic text, *Be'er Mayyim Hayyim* (*Well of Living Waters*) by Rabbi Hayyim of Chernovitz.

At the conclusion of the Sabbath, I accompanied

Rabbi and Mrs. Gertner to a meeting in Queens with a group of American *ba'alei teshuvah* (returnees to the Jewish tradition) interested in founding a community somewhere upstate. Zanvil, owner of a thriving kosher dairy business, would be able to provide a means of support. This could be a marriage of convenience: The young couples needed financial underwriting for their ideal. Zanvil, on the other hand, needed recruits to populate the hasidic community he had long dreamed of. The men and women seated around him on the living room floor might possibly become the first generation of a new utopia.

Moshe, the spokesman for the *ba'alei teshuvah*—who with his dark good looks, beret, and beard might have passed for Che Guevara's brother—said they were looking for a rural setting yet not too far removed from the great rebbes in New York, the Lubavitch Rebbe and the Satmar Rebbe. Zanvil submitted they would have to hire a *melamed* (religious instructor) to teach their children.

In the car ride back to their Williamsburg, Brooklyn home, the Gertners discussed the level of modesty of the women's dress. One of the women's hair had not been fully covered by her kerchief. Something else bothered them about the interviewees—their obviously high regard for the Lubavitcher Rebbe.

"Did you ever hear of a *zaddik* who makes himself a birthday party?"

As the hour was late, I accepted my hosts' gracious offer to put me up Saturday night in their Williamsburg flat. Zanvil was on the phone to Israel. The word "cartel" kept coming up. I knew he could not have been referring to the oil cartel—but then to what was he alluding?

At the time there was no way I could have known that Zanvil Gertner was something of a celebrity in zealot circles. In the early sixties, when ten year old Israeli Yossele Shumacher was kidnapped at his Orthodox grandfather's behest to prevent his parents (recently arrived from Russia) from secularizing him—an escapade that involved Rabbi Amram Blau's wife Ruth, a French convert to Judaism, and Rabbi Moshe Soloveichik of Lucerne, Switzerland, among others—his final stop was the Williamsburg home of Zanvil Gertner. It was there Yossele was finally nabbed by FBI agents after a pact was reached between the Mossad's Isser Harel and then U. S. Attorney General Robert Kennedy. Zanvil, I found out, was an adherent of one of the tiniest hasidic groups known as the *Malokhim* (Angels). Back in the thirties, an impressionable Zanvil Gertner had come under the sway of a Lubavitcher hasid, Rabbi Hayyim Abraham Dov Baer Hakohen Levine, whose charisma was such that he became a mentor in his own right. To this day, his followers refer to him simply as "the *Malakh*," the Angel.

Rabbi Joseph Isaac Schneersohn
[1880-1950]

A Look Back

IT IS A JEWISH CUSTOM TO VISIT THE CEMETERY during the month of *Ellul* to ready oneself for the approaching Days of Awe. I felt I needed this preparation. I also wanted to behold with my own eyes the final resting place of the last Lubavitcher Rebbe, Menahem Mendel Schneerson. Call it a spectator's curiosity.

The Rebbe is buried in Montefiore Cemetery, located in Cambria Heights, Queens, a black neighborhood. It is not difficult to find the spot. Signs placed strategically, starting at the street, direct the visitor "to the *Ohel*" (Hebrew for "tent," by which the hasidim refer to the Rebbe's tomb). At the street entrance, a table has been set up for pilgrims to sit and write their *pidyon*, a formal request or petition to be read by the supplicant at the *Ohel*. A *pidyon* might include a list of names of loved ones in need of blessing. Or it might assume a more informal tone: "Less stress," reads one scrap of paper in the pile.

In the antechamber adjoining the graves, provisions have been made for the lighting of memorial tapers. Before entering the actual open-air tomb, hasidim remove their shoes.

A generation ago, I visited the grave of the "Freerdicker Rebbe" (Previous Rebbe), as he was called in those days—Joseph Isaac Schneersohn. Today, next to his monument is that of his son-in-law, the Rebbe I "knew," if one can use the word for a relationship that admitted no intimacy. The wording of the two tombstones is almost exactly identical, the one deviation being that Rabbi Menahem Mendel is described as a *gaon* (genius), as is Rabbi Shalom Dov Baer, Joseph Isaac's father, but not Joseph Isaac himself. If one comes expecting any hint of a Messianic role, one will be sorely disappointed. In generations to come, based on the data provided on the stone, there will be no indication that this is the man many once believed to be the Messiah.

The faithful—men, women and children—stand facing the markers, reading *Ma'aneh Lashon*, a small collection of Psalms and other prayers assembled by the *Mitteler Rebbe* to be read at the grave of his father, the founder of Habad, in Hoditz, Russia. At a certain point, the pilgrim will read his *pidyon*, and having concluded the reading, tear it to bits, throwing it into a large holding area over the graves. Eventually, the thousands of notes to heaven will be gathered up and cremated in the furnace outdoors. The incessant smoke of the furnace causes me to gag. Based on the deliberation with which my neighbors rip up their *pidyonos*, great psychic energy would appear to be invested in the ritual act.

Surrounding the *Ohel* on all sides, are the relatives and most devoted followers of the rebbes, but the focus is clearly on the leaders themselves. I ask a hasid standing outside the *Ohel*, where the grave of Rabbi Nissan Telushkin, a prominent rabbi, is located. He shrugs me away.

The small home adjoining the Lubavitch section of the cemetery has been purchased by the movement as a caretaker's house, funds provided by the patron of worldwide Habad activities, Australian philanthropist Rabbi Joseph Gutnick. It contains an ark so prayers may be conducted there. A man is foraging through the books in a state of disarray on the shelf. I ask him what he is looking for.

"*Igrois*." A volume of the Rebbe's letters.

He complains that since the remodeling it is impossible to find anything here. I help him to find a volume of the Rebbe's teachings, which among other

The graves of Rabbis Joseph Isaac Schneersohn
and Menahem Mendel Schneerson.

items, contains several letters. "That will work," he thanks me.

Since the Rebbe's passing, this is the way to receive a written reply to pressing questions. The page one flips open to, is the message. Outside on a bench he reads to his wife, a woman in an agitated state, the letter intended for them.

On the walkway next to the small building, a table is replete with cookies and a hot water urn for coffee and tea. I grab a cookie.

On the way out to the street, I pass well-dressed arrivals whose livery indicates they have come straight from JFK Airport. Two weeks later, the media would give extensive coverage to the pilgrimage of visiting Israeli Prime Minister Benjamin Netanyahu.

Epilogue

And the earth was void and desolate, and darkness was upon the face of the deep, ***and the spirit of God was hovering over the face of the waters***" (Genesis).
"*This is the spirit of King Messiah*" (Midrash).

THERE ARE TIMES IN HISTORY WHEN THE DISEMBODIED spirit of Messiah gravitates toward a human being, when the longing of aeons upon aeons begins to concatenate in flesh-and-blood. The figure casts its net wide, becoming the collective face of a generation, its features reflected in the waves of humanity.

And then that body comes to its mortal end, and the Messianic spirit once again becomes precisely that, a spirit, a longing for Messiah. "The spirit of King Messiah hovering."

And the generation that had felt fluttering about it mighty wings, wings of Messiah aroused from his nest to sweep Israel up from the Void, from desolation, from darkness, from the abyss—is consigned once more to waiting, comforted in the knowledge that the transcendental spirit is also an immanent spirit; that *Yehidah*, the Oversoul of us all, is also the individual soul of each and every one of us; that the great bird of freedom is in reality a great, ancient flying fish, Rav Ham-nuna Saba of the *Zohar*, seen streaking "over the face of the waters."

GLOSSARY

(Unless otherwise stated, all entries are Hebrew.)

Alter Rebbe ~ (Yiddish) literally "Old Rabbi," Rabbi Shneur Zalman of Liady (1745-1813), founder of Habad Hasidism

Ashkenazi(c), pertaining to Ashkenazim, European Jews of German descent

atsvut ~ sadness

Baal Shem Tov ~ Rabbi Israel Baal Shem Tov (1698 or 1700-1760), founder of Eastern European Hasidism

Baal ha-Tanya ~ author of *Tanya*, Rabbi Shneur Zalman of Liady

baal tefillah ~ master of prayer, prayer leader

ba'alei teshuvah (pl. baalei teshuvah) ~ returnee to Jewish tradition

baal tokeya ~ one who sounds the *shofar* or ram's horn

Baruch Ber ~ Rabbi Baruch Dov Leibowitz (1864-1940), head of the Kamenetz Yeshiva, Lithuania; preeminent Talmudist of his day

bikkurim ~ first fruits offered to the priest in the Holy Temple

bobbe ~ (Yiddish) grandmother

davennen ~ (Yiddish) praying

Erets Yisrael ~ Land of Israel

farbrengen ~ (Yiddish) hasidic gathering

gabbai ~ attendant (of rebbe)

galut ~ exile, either cosmic, collective, or individual

gaon ~ talmudic genius

Gaon of Vilna – see Vilna Gaon

gashmiyut ~ physicality

Gerer ~ pertaining to Ger or Gur, Yiddish for Gora Kalwaria, Poland; a branch of Polish hasidism founded by R. Isaac Meir of Gur

ger zedek ~ righteous convert to Judaism

gevaldig ~ (Yiddish) extraordinary, wonderful

HaBaD ~ acrostic for *hokhmah, binah, daat* (wisdom, understanding, knowledge), motto of the branch of hasidism founded by Rabbi Shneur Zalman of Liady at the end of the eighteenth century

habadnik ~ follower of Habad hasidism

Hafets Hayyim ~ Rabbi Israel Meir Kagan (1838-1933), saintly leader of his generation, so-called after the title of his book on laws of slander

halacha ~ Jewish Law

hamets ~ leavened bread forbidden on Passover

hashgocho protis ~ divine supervision

hasid (pl. hasidim) ~ adherent of movement founded by Rabbi Israel Baal Shem Tov

Haskalah ~ movement for secular enlightenment among Jews of Europe, anathema to Hasidim

Hazon Ish ~ author of halachic work by that name, Rabbi Abraham Isaiah Karelitz (1879-1952) of Vilna and later B'nai Berak, Israel

hevrah kadisha ~ burial society

huppah ~ wedding canopy

iluy ~ prodigy

Kabbalah ~ Jewish Mysticism

kelipah ~ literally "husk," the realm of impurity

kiddush ~ an aperitif with religious significance

kittel ~ (Yiddish) white robe worn by men on Yom Kippur and at the Passover seder table; also serves as burial shroud

kohen ~ member of the priestly class descended from Aaron

maamar (pl. maamorim) ~ a hasidic discourse of a mystical nature

mamash ~ really

mashpi'a ~ teacher of Habad Hasidism, also spiritual supervisor of a Habad yeshiva

mazal ~ luck

melamed ~ religious instructor of children

merirut ~ bitterness

meshulach (pl. meshulachim) ~ fund raiser

mikveh ~ ritual bath

Mishnah ~ code of Jewish Law completed in Israel circa 200 C.E. by Rabbi Judah the Prince

misnaged (pl. misnagdim) ~ opponent of Hasidism, follower of Rabbi Elijah, the Gaon of Vilna

mitsvah ~ commandment, good deed

Mitteler Rebbe ~ (Yiddish) "Middle Rabbi," Rabbi Dov Baer Shneuri (1774-1828), son of founder of Habad hasidism

moshav ~ cooperative settlement

mukhtar ~ (Arabic) mayor

Mussar ~ Lithuanian ethical movement founded by Rabbi Israel Lipkin (1810-1883), known as Rabbi Israel Salanter after his birthplace, Salant

mussarnik ~ follower of Myssar movement

narish ~ (Yiddish) foolish

niggun (pl. niggunim) ~ hasidic tune

nistar ~ hidden person

Ohel ~ "tent," the word hasidim use for the rebbe's tomb

'oved Hashem ~ one who serves God

parochet ~ curtain covering holy ark in synagogue

payos ~ sideburns worn by Orthodox men in observance of Leviticus 19:27

pidyon (plural pidyonos) ~ a formal request or petition to be read by the supplicant at the *Ohel*

pravven golus ~ (Yiddish) to self-impose exile

RaSHaB ~ initials of Rabbi Shalom Baer of Lubavitch (1861-1920), fifth rebbe of Schneersohn dynasty

rebbe (pl. rebbeim) ~ hasidic master

Rosh Yeshiva ~ dean of yeshiva, talmudic academy

ruchniyut ~ spirituality

Sabbatianism ~ messianic movement founded by Shabbetai Zevi, the seventeeth-century Turkish mystic

schmuess ~ (Yiddish) to chat

schnorrer ~ (Yiddish) beggar

schule ~ (Yiddish) synagogue

Sefardim ~ Jews of Spanish or Arab lands

sefer ~ a sacred book

semicha ~ rabbinic ordination

Shaar ha-Kollel ~ halachic commentary on Lubavitch prayer book by Rabbi Abraham David Lavoot of Nikolayev

shaliach ~ emissary (of Lubavitcher Rebbe)

Shavuot ~ Festival of Pentecost

she'elah ~ question of Jewish law

shehitah ~ ritual slaughter

Shekhinah ~ Divine presence or indwelling

shelihut ~ mission (for Lubavitcher Rebbe)

shiur ~ talmudic lecture

shofar ~ ram's horn

shtiebel ~ (Yiddish) Hasidic synagogue in homey, informal setting

taharah ~ ritual washing of corpse

tallis ~ prayer shawl

talmid (pl. talmidim) ~ student

Talmud ~ corpus of Jewish Law comprising Mishnah and Gemara

Tanya ~ basic text of Habad Hasidism, written by Rabbi Shneur Zalman of Liady, Russia, end eighteenth century

TaZ ~ acrostic for *Turei Zahav*, commentary on *Shulhan Arukh*; also author of work by that name, Rabbi David Halevy (circa 1586-1667)

tefillin ~ small leather boxes containing scriptural passages worn on the left arm and forehead during morning weekday prayers

tevillah ~ ritual immersion

tisch ~ (Yiddish) literally "table," hasidic gathering

Tosafot ~ commentary to Talmud by medieval French rabbis

Trisker Maggid ~ Rabbi Abraham Twersky (1806-1889), *maggid* or preacher of Turisk; third generation rebbe of the Chernobyl dynasty

Vilna Gaon ~ R. Elijah of Vilna (1720-1797), the greatest opponent of Hasidism

yahrzeit ~ annual observance of day of death

yehidah ~ according to kabbalistic teaching, the highest level of the soul, the Oversoul

yehidut ~ private audience with rebbe

yeshiva ~ talmudic academy

yeshiva bachur ~ student of a yeshiva

yom tov ~ festival

Yud Tes Kislev ~ 19th of Hebrew month of Kislev, celebration of liberation of the Alter Rebbe from czarist imprisonment

zaddik (pl. zaddikim) ~ righteous person

zeide ~ (Yiddish) grandfather

Zemah Zedek ~ author of halachic work by that title, Rabbi Menahem Mendel I of Lubavitch (1789-1866), grandson of the Alter Rebbe, Rabbi Shneur Zalman of Liady

Zohar ~ classic text of the Kabbalah

White Cloud Press publishes books on religion, mythology, and memoirs. To receive a free catalog or more information on our books, please contact us at:

White Cloud Press
PO Box 3400
Ashland, Oregon
Phone/fax: 1-800-380-8286
website: http://www/jeffnet.org/whitecloud